*how to really know yourself
through your handwriting*

how to really know yourself through your handwriting

Shirl Solomon

TAPLINGER PUBLISHING COMPANY | NEW YORK

First Edition

Published in the United States in 1973 by
TAPLINGER PUBLISHING CO., INC.
New York, New York

Published simultaneously in the Dominion of Canada by
Burns & MacEachern, Ltd., Toronto

Library of Congress Catalog Card Number: 72-8321

ISBN 0-8008-3966-8

Designed by Mollie M. Torras

To my children
CINDY, MARK *and* **LORI**
who helped me to grow along with them
and gave me deeper vision.
Their willingness to express to me
their unfolding personalities
with innocent faith
reassured me that the search for
a more profound understanding of the child
and the adult is worth the struggle.
The search can be the beginning of love.

contents

8 *contents*

preface

This book is about you and your handwriting. It will help you to know yourself in all your facets and allow you to meet the total person you are. With this new discovery you will also gain an understanding and insight into the core of other people, see them with new vision and be able to develop a sounder basis for your attitudes toward them.

You will learn how to ferret out the unconscious mechanisms which work within you and relate them to your conscious attitudes and behavior, learn why they exist and why they have been repressed. You will then have the advantage of being able to remove the mental blocks which interfere with greater self-realization. The choice then becomes yours to follow one of three courses, any of which will prove ultimately more satisfying than uncontrolled compulsive actions:

1. Free yourself of destructive compulsions and attitudes.
2. Change them into something positive.
3. Recognize their existence and thus be better able to control and live with them.

Life is a onetime gift. It is intended to be realized to its fullest.

When you finally arrive at the reality that true fulfillment and gratification come only from what you give of yourself and in return what you receive from yourself that you begin to enjoy and be comfortable with life. Family, friends, and loved ones contribute to joys and sorrows and are important in the world of each human being. However, no matter how dearly loved they are, the reality is that your primary responsibility is to justify your own life by nurturing it to full growth.

Your natural abilities, strengths, talents, mind, and emotions were given to you to be used and developed. When they are not given the opportunity to act in accordance with their performance level, they weaken and lose their natural potential. If these qualities are not exercised at all, they will atrophy and become nonfunctioning. You will be led to believe that they never existed, for in your conscious mind they do not. You may be living half a life—or even less. You are not only depriving yourself, but you are also depriving others of what you could be for yourself and for them. Greater awareness and appreciation for being will arouse enthusiasm to nurture those small seedlings with which you were endowed and allow them to blossom forth. As self-worth increases so does the value of what you have to offer others, and as you become more content and happier with yourself, your capacity to give happiness is enhanced.

The key to opening the front door is first to remove all the outer gear and look with honest eyes at your total nakedness. Then you will concentrate on each separate part, understanding its particular function and applying your own life experience to why it behaves the way it does. To complete the process relate these separate parts to one another, observe how they interact and perform together as one total body. This book is a study of you, unmasked.

You begin as the physical child, where learning experience first takes place. These early impressions, imitations, and attitudes were highly significant in determining you, the adult. You will be able to recognize in your handwriting any childhood traits which never matured. They may appear as positive rather than negative traits, but it will be important that you see and evaluate them. Throughout this study you, the child, will accompany you, the adult. You exist together, and whether or not you are aware of it, this coexistence continues along the entire journey of life. Hopefully, the adult is in command, even while learning from the child and enjoying the naïve and unsaturated pleasures felt through the child. Don't resent or reject the child. Try to understand and to like him. It's the only way you can move toward liking yourself.

People are often confounded when they are asked who they are, and they will most frequently reply by describing a social state of being; such as their nationality, religion, profession, sex, and marital status. Some people will reply, "I am me," "I am myself," or "I am a human being." This is their way of indicating to the interrogator that they are more than can be answered by a name or a label. You may be more, but at the least you are a physical, mental, emotional, and social being. In one word a—personality, unique in your combination of characteristics. You may identify in many ways with other people and have striking resemblances to physical and behavioristic traits. However, there is nobody just like you in the whole world, and it is the differences which make you an individual personality.

Personality is born when you are, since its existence is only meaningful in interaction with the world outside the self. From the begining you strive to be an independent body, for even though you have help you are pushing your way out of a warm, protective shelter to an alien world where you must immediately contribute to your survival. Once the cord is cut and you are slapped soundly on the buttocks, you are on your own to breathe in free air and feel the blood circulate in its own system. Let's look at the circumstances of your original exposure to the outside world. You are slapped, you cry and are able to breathe and get the blood circulating on its own. You cry again, and this time you are fed, burped, or diaper changed. Not much later you recognize that by crying you will get responses from other people. Mother will cuddle and rock you, holding you close to her breast where you are warm and comfortable. Someone will give you a toy to play with. Sooner or later crying will give you the attention you want. This early memory of provoking responses from others by crying is so strong in later life that, if a healthy transition is not made, you will cry outwardly (or resulting in even more damage, inwardly) for the things you want given to you. Bitterness and frustration will be felt when your cries are unheeded, because your childhood memory traces have continued and you expect the same responses you received as a child.

Love is an ever-changing concept during the various stages of the developing human being. The first association with a love feeling is little more than the satisfying of basic needs, and is most evident in infants and growing children who are dependent upon their parents and feel love in terms of being protected and taken care of. A natural outgrowth of securing the basic needs is the desire to gain acceptance and approval. Demonstrations of affection and devotion are often bestowed upon others with the prime purpose of being able to feel wanted. While these motives are the foundation for a growing love concept, there is a simultaneous interplay of the pleasure principle which greatly influences and sometimes conflicts with the desire for security and acceptance. However, we should accept as fact that there can be no love without pleasure. The most mature stage is to identify with another human being with a desire to exchange pleasures and to help each other achieve both your needs. The mature adult should be able to give and receive all of these things, though he may arrive at each level at different stages of his development. Few people have a mature understanding of the love concept. They prefer to view love as something very personal and different to each individual. It is personal and different for those involved in a one-to-one relationship, but it can only be complete with the awareness and desire of both to respond to the full love need of each other. Unfortunately, too many adults do not move through the entire cycle. As a result, many relationships are unsatisfying, incomplete, or total disasters.

At this point I wish to reemphasize the structure of the love concept, as it is an important tenet for personality evaluation.

1. The desire to satisfy basic needs (food, shelter, sex).
2. Need for acceptance and approval from the home and society.
3. The desire and pursuit of pleasure.
4. The ability to identify your own desires and needs with those of others and gain satisfaction from exchanging with them.

If this concept of love is accepted by you, then it must be your ultimate goal in life, for it includes every need and personal desire. To be expressed and realized it must be mirrored by another or other human beings, for all but the basic needs was learned from them. The struggle to attain a profound love is behind all the great efforts of man. He rarely finds it in one person, for though two people may basically want the same things in life, they don't look for them in the same ways. This difference is important because it creates a bridge separating people, who really want the same things but have developed other ideas in how to achieve them. Opposites may attract, but they don't make for a happy union. Similarity of thought and feeling is what helps one person to identify and exchange with another, allowing them both to move toward fulfilling the whole love concept. The child is not capable of either feeling or expressing this high level of love, but an early awareness of himself in relation to other people will provide a foundation from which to climb to higher levels.

You, the mature adult, accept and approve of your child self the same as you do of the child born to you. If you do not, you are rejecting a part of your personality. Young children about you will often trigger off memories of your own attitudes and reactions at their age, but it is important that you realize that many of these childhood attitudes are still influencing you. Some may have a negative effect, but many attitudes have kept the door open for fun and play. When you can still identify as a child with a real child, you have the capacity to empathize and respond meaningfully with the understanding of both a child and an adult. Further, if you are acting out the complete love concept, you can place the child at what you believe to be his level and relate to him with that knowledge in mind. You may not wish to play this role with adult associations where child levels of love are dominant, and unfortunately this state of underdevelopment persists with many people right to the grave. A well-adjusted personality accepts himself in each stage of development and seeks to establish near equal associations with other people. His objectives and goals in life are motivated by the need for self-expression, and his full love concept creates in him the desire to enhance that same expression in the one he chooses to love. Though many may claim that love is blind or something that just happens, emotional feelings and reactions can be traced back to their origin, which begins with the image of mother and then father. From there on exists a broad range of influencing images, but the adult must accept the responsibility of his choices and the emotional commitments he makes to them.

The adult does not cry in frustration over failures or not attaining certain desires, like the child who doesn't know what else to do but to cry. The mature mind separates passion from reason, seeing the effort as a failure but not himself. If the desire is sufficiently intense, he will review the aspects leading to failure and set out again, but this time equipped with new knowledge and a change in approach. Continuation of failure is often the result of trying again and again in the exact same way, like trying over and over again to thread a needle in the dark without taking the time to switch on the light.

Most significant about the mature personality is the ability it has to relate to many different roles. Vast exposure to images of child, parent, teacher, friend, lover, employer, husband, wife, leader, and follower expand the ability of the personality to operate on many different levels. Because of this flexibility, the personality is capable of coping with most situations. It can project into any one of the roles mentioned, and those that haven't been, and yet be more dynamically individual than the personality limited to one role at a time.

What you have to offer yourself is inestimable. You haven't begun to tap the true potential. As you begin to do so, others will also benefit by the value of your increased growth.

The hand is the instrument of the brain. It is obedient and follows instructions conveyed to it. Anyone taking the time to observe the action of the hands of someone speaking will note that they frequently move about describing and painting pictures along with the vocalized expressions. At a boxing match, spectators will clench their fists and even start swinging their arms wildly while watching the bout. People who are listening to music will often tap their fingers in time to the beat. At concerts I have even observed someone in the audience waving an imaginary baton. At a chess tournament many players rub their foreheads constantly or press their hands against the temple, for better concentration. These are small revelations which tell something about the person, or about what he is feeling at the time he is being observed. You glean other small impressions upon meeting people by their manner of dress, the way they shake your hand (or don't), facial expressions, and their tone of voice, together with what they say. We sometimes get the opportunity after the first meeting to learn that our original impressions were wrong. This should not come as a surprise, as the impressions were based on surface factors and conditions prevailing at the time of the meeting, which also influence our judgments as well as the other person's behavior.

Writing with the hand is an action which relies upon all your faculties. The force of your physical, mental, emotional, and spiritual expression is combined in this one act. Even the slightest hand contraction will be evidenced in the writing. When the mind relaxes, so does the hand moving with the pen across the page. When the emotions are tense and the mind is strained, the fingers will grip the writing tool with muscular tension and move with greater effort. In observing this symbiosis of brain and hand through the handwriting, remarkable discoveries have been made. These discoveries have been clarified not only by the writer, himself (who is often not aware or willing to admit them), but also by authoritative reports from schools, medical and psychology sources, employment records, and judicial courts.

As a child you first began to doodle and draw before ever attempting to reproduce letters, which require discipline and control. However, we must go back even further to learn what faculties had to be developed in order to succeed in the act of writing.

The one-month embryo shows the brain, eyes, and hands already taking form. When the infant is born, normal development is measured by his ability at the expected stage to bring objects into focus with his eyes and then to reach out with his hands for the objects in view. When he is able to grasp, he then begins to manipulate with the fingers, and when he can hold objects in both hands he can then begin to bring them into action in an upward and downward motion. This is not learned, but a natural development process of mind and body. However, refinement and greater agility in the function of the brain-eye-hand complex is later very much influenced by learning and emotional experiences. No matter how well coordinated, a child who is emotionally upset will have difficulty with handwriting. There is a very real way that the graphologist can be of value, as he can almost immediately spot an emotional problem which may be holding a child back from normal or even exceptional progress. Even with a child whose coordination develops slowly, it is not necessarily an indication that later progress will be consistent with these early signs. Certain environmental influences, together with intense motivation, have shown some of these children to grow into high achievers later in life. A child may not be particularly adaptive to writing principles in his early stages of learning, but as he develops, so will his handwriting.

When you first attended school, you were allowed and encouraged to use your hands freely in pasting, inkblot drawings, and coloring. Then when taught about letters and told to reproduce them with pencil and paper, you started out slowly and cautiously, holding your fingers tightly on the pencil, very close to the point. You made large movements, but once familiar and more confident with this exercise, you began to reduce the size of the letters and increase your speed. You were learning to read at the same time, and anxious to form word thoughts like "I, me, Dad, Mom, house, love." Later you were introduced to modified printing, using different-size letters and zones of writing. This was an arduous and trying exercise, as now you had to think harder, remember much more and move into other areas of space. At this point, if you were not happy at home or had some problem bothering you, this additional demand upon you was strongly felt and your writing performance suffered. If the home or personal problem continued when you approached cursive (connected) writing, your writing showed an even greater strain. Many adults claim that they have always printed because their handwriting was so poor, without attempting to remember the conditions prevailing when as a child they were being taught cursive writing.

Throughout your school years, writing was a major tool for learning and in proving your worth as a student. Homework, compositions, written examinations were not only implements for learning, but they were also proof that you were carrying out your responsibilities both to school and family. The degree to which you feel and carry out your obligations is reflected in your handwriting, as well as how well you have learned to exercise your thinking and the attitudes acquired along the way.

The roots of your personality may well be fairly set shortly after the age of five, but the obvious changes which occur in puberty and adolescence are considerable, and restructuring often takes place at these two later stages with the strong influence of the small child. The adult personality is difficult to change, but not impossible. What a task it would be to break down even a shaky foundation, and rebuild it differently with the same materials. If it were weak to begin with, the years would not have made it stronger without adding supports and stabilizers. The answer is to add supports and stabilizers to the same personality, removing the locks and opening the windows, letting in the healthy elements of the outside world. You will look and feel different, the same personality aired out with a stronger hold on itself, when you are able to make these changes rather than tear down everything you are and try to begin over again.

In this study you are being challenged to face up to yourself, what you were, are, and can become. You will be constantly retracing your childhood and will come to understand how particular feelings and attitudes became implanted and remained with you though you find them undesirable to present living. As you become more conditioned and less threatened when you look closer at yourself, your vision will improve and you will have access to opening doors never before opened.

This is an exciting adventure with the assured outcome that you will be a winner. Keep an open mind, submit to all the tests given, and apply each graphological principle to your own handwriting. At the end of each chapter, you will be asked to score yourself in the area provided. When you have completed the entire book, you should record all your findings on the personality evaluation sheet. Many of the examples of handwriting are exaggerated in their peculiarities so that you can see them more clearly. You will have to judge for yourself the degree of any characteristics which apply to you, but don't ignore the small and more subtle handwriting indices.

You will probably need to review some chapters to reconsider your true results, as it will be natural that you tend to reject some characteristics displeasing to you. The value of this work for you is as great as your ability to be honest and sincere, no matter how painful. The happy discoveries will act as a buffer for the less pleasing ones you are sure to encounter.

Give consideration to the chapter "How You Can Change." Remember, a negative can be turned into a positive. First, you must be willing to see it.

Good luck.

how to really know yourself
through your handwriting

1.

your motivation symbols

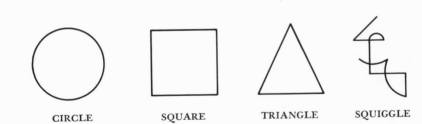

| CIRCLE | SQUARE | TRIANGLE | SQUIGGLE |

Here are four geometric forms. Which one pleases your eye the most? Record below your first preference, the one you like second best, your third choice and the one which appeals to you the least.

1. _____

2. _____

3. _____

4. _____

These symbols are explained in the following pages. It is important that you thoroughly understand them, as they are the basic forms of letter writing. They will be referred to frequently during this study.

To confirm your choice, take a sample of your own handwriting and see which of the above forms, in part or whole, appear most frequently. If they are consistent with the order of your selection above, you may freely accept the explanations outlined in the text. Your writing forms need not be exact in appearance to the symbols, but they must follow the general pattern of movement.

There are reasons for your choice.

THE CIRCLE

The circle is the LOVE symbol. If you selected it as your first preference, you are most motivated by love. This round form will appear frequently in the *o*'s, *a*'s, *e*'s, *g*'s, upper and lower loops, and the letter-ending strokes of your handwriting, as demonstrated below.

$$\sigma\quad a\quad e\quad g\quad \ell\quad f\quad k\quad p\quad g\quad m$$

To understand why it is referred to as the love symbol, we now recall the child to see what his concept of love is. In the small child's mind, love is pleasure, and things that are round, soft, and warm please him. A rattle, a ball, and a mother's warm breasts are a comfort and delight. There are no sharp edges which can hurt. He responds to round objects which soothe, pacify, and provide safe play.

If you are still attached to the round form, then love, camaraderie, and playfulness are most urgently behind your attitudes and behavior. You abhor violence, run away from a street brawl, shudder at the sight of an accident, and find arguments distressing and distasteful. What you seek mostly is affection and approval, which you find in situations of play rather than competitive achievement. If the circle is almost exclusively used in your handwriting, you foster practically no resentment toward others (except where your love interests are threatened). You are neither hostile nor aggressive. In short, you would rather play than fight.

When circles appear as accouterments and additions to the letter, rather than as part of the basic form, your love is self-indulgent. You tend to be possessive and jealous about people and things which give you pleasure. Here are examples of desire for self-pleasure with a possessive and jealous hold on it.

On some levels you will share because you are playful and want attention from others, but your giving is limited to the assurance that you will get more than you give. Those small extra circles close off to others the things you want to keep for yourself and you will not share them. The child in you is still saying, "I want it for myself, it's mine!"

THE SQUARE

The square is the SECURITY symbol. In choosing it as your first preference, you are mostly motivated by the desire for security. For verification, look to see how often this form appears in your sample writing. It is most evident in the letters *h, m, n, r, p, u,* and *w,* as shown below.

You were introduced to the square shape the first time you were placed in a crib as an infant. It kept you safe and secure. Later, you were put into a playpen which was larger, but still square and protected from harm. Blocks were given to you to play with, and as you became more intelligent, you started to place one on top of the other, building structures. As you progressed further and took to doodling and drawing, a square shape invariably took the form of a house. In the square house lived mother, father, and you. This was your security. You play house and play adult, simulating the role of a parent.

You, as the security-motivated individual, find your home to be your castle. Whether it is gardening, taking care of repairs and improvements, entertaining in the home or generally puttering around, you are comfortable and content in a home situation. You also like working with your hands and have a mind that likes to build on things. The quality of patience helps you to follow through each step of a project until a desired result is achieved.

You are both logical and practical, accumulating information and ideas you feel can be useful to you. Abstract thinking is beyond you and you do not indulge in romantic and idealistic philosophies. You are guided by the desire to build and secure a strong foundation, and then live in it. Though some people may refer to you as square, they should be reminded that solid people such as you are the ones who can be counted on.

THE TRIANGLE

The triangle is the SEX symbol. It is a pointed wedge shape which can push further and release greater energy than any other form. At a study made at Yale University Child Development Clinic, it was observed that the triangle was a more developed stage of the brain, eye, and hand complex. The normal child did not draw this form until the age of five, though the circle and square were accomplished at three and four years of age. If, as a child, you selected triangular shapes to play with, you were aggressive and energetic. You were willing to chance the danger of this pointed shape so that you might poke, probe, and dig. Your pleasures in play were the satisfying of curiosity and releasing energy. In drawings you would have depicted church steeples, pointed rooftops, airplanes, sailboats, and triangular trees. Even what would be considered a round form would have the triangular characteristic, like fingers, feet, and a pointed head.

Experiments at Yale University and at McGill University in Montreal have indicated that emotions are affected by the action in the hypothalamus in the center of the brain. By electrically stimulating this portion of the brain, responses of love, hate, fear, aggressiveness, and sex have been evoked. Aggressiveness is closely identified with the sex urge, since they both produce a high degree of excitation and seek active outlets for this energy. If, as a child or adult, you were not able to satisfy one of these urges, you would have tried to replace it with the other.

Sigmund Freud makes reference to the triangle as being a phallic symbol, representing the sexual organs of the male and the female. In dream interpretation, many objects have sexual implications, such as a knife, gun, airplane, elevator, and so on. Their particular significance, of course, is related to the dream sequence itself and the dreamer. Many psychoanalysts believe that the sexual instinct is the most powerful generator of excitation. Because of this it is also the greatest contributor to neurosis when this energy is not healthfully liberated.

The body seeks to get all its parts into action and to keep them moving at a pace that neither strains nor underworks them. The degree to which you lend your emotional enthusiasm and motivation is the degree of aggressiveness in your personality. Aggression against yourself and others is a result of thwarting this energy or not channeling it properly. It needs a healthy release so that hostility, asocial behavior, withdrawal, and ill health will not occur. Properly directed, the aggressive personality will prove dynamic and achieve great satisfactions, not only for the self, but also for the society.

If you selected the triangle as your first choice, you will be able to clarify it as your true motivation symbol by the wedge shapes and points appearing in the following letters:

M M A A A M M M

The extent to which you are determined to follow through with dynamic action is indicated by the height of these points and wedges. The higher they are, the greater is your need for outward realization and the more you desire the world to recognize your achievements. Your triangular letters show you to have sharpness of thought and keen perception. You want to arrive at solutions quickly. Therefore, you travel by the shortest, most direct route. You resent wasting time and are impatient with others whose slower thinking impedes your own progress. You are an independent thinker who resists being placed in any subordinate position to others, as you like to work independently and have the ability to do so. You are curious and exploring, producing ideas and solving problems while leaving the burdensome details to be carried out by others more equipped for smaller and less inventive tasks. Your efforts and energies are directed toward making a success of a project by your mental acuity and prowess, and are bored with the smaller incidental aspects which do not present a challenge.

Though you can be extremely emotional, and even explosive, you are not too personally involved with other people. The pleasures you might derive from sharing work, play, and goals take a back seat to your drive for achievement on a personal level. Therefore, you are not particularly sensitive or compassionate to the emotional needs of others. However, when you do extend yourself, the value and quality of what you do have to give is of high measure. You react quickly and perceptively in an emergency without losing control. You do not give vent to pettiness and haggling, nor waste time in too much small talk. You are direct, bent on getting to the point quickly, and then on to the next things.

Most people like and admire you—from a distance. They are afraid to approach you on an intimate basis. You present a threat to their feelings of inadequacy and self-imposed limitations, but inwardly they would like to be more like you.

You, the triangle-motivated person, can be a dynamic producer who can contribute greatly to yourself and the environment. You also have the potential to be destructive, if your abounding energy takes a misguided direction. You will read later what pitfalls should be avoided and what changes can be made if you have already taken steps on a dangerous road. If you haven't gone too far, you can still retrace your steps and find the right path.

SQUIGGLE

The squiggle is the IMAGINATION symbol. It is the only one of the four forms which is unfamiliar. By combining all the other shapes it creates a design of its own. When you do the same thing in your handwriting, you are using your imagination. Your configurations may not look like the squiggle, but they will have added to them something new and creative which reflect your unique personality. Here are some examples of minds which perceive something more or in a different way, and they express it in these letter forms:

Your imagination is spurred on by an insatiable desire to see and know more. When you receive images, your imagination will stretch your mind to envision more. Not satisfied in accepting only what is known, you search for the unknown. You are curious and have the ability to form progressive thought patterns which lead you to create something new and personal. You expand on the things you learn and observe, contributing your vision and insight.

You are not always in touch with reality. Much of your thinking time is spent in loftier thought beyond the mundane existence of everyday living. In the exclusiveness of your imagination, you will romanticize, fantasize, philosophize, and spiritualize, and enjoy the fullness this adds to your life. If you are also aggressive, as indicated in the triangle form, you will use your imagination as a valuable tool to achieve success which will give you greater comfort and luxury in social living. If no triangular movements appear in your writing, you are a visionary with aesthetic values. You do not search for rewards of a material nature nor do you direct your special talents to that end. The satisfaction you gain is just from the joy of finding outlets for this inner expression and the opportunity to use your gift of imagination.

If you have, unfortunately, for whatever reasons, suppressed this natural ability to be imaginative in an active sense, you are probably experiencing some of the negative consequences. When there is no channeling of this energy into an active source but it is instead pushed back or cut off, the effect on the personality may be withdrawal, neuroticism, or aggression. Many imaginative people who lack the initiative to move ahead and materialize their visions will find secondary or tertiary outlets to maintain their balance and sanity. This may be found in teaching the ideas and creations of others, working with unusual children and thus feeling this expression vicariously, or becoming involved in hobbies which provide at least the partial outlet needed. Frequently, parents will concentrate all their efforts toward developing a particular talent in their child as a way of sublimating their own need for personal expression.

As a strongly motivated individual with the need to express your ability to create, you reject routine, punching a time clock, punctuality, protocol, superficial conversations, and the sameness of activity. You are not a social status seeker, a joiner of groups, or a partygoer. You measure the value of people and things by their intrinsic worth rather than by surface or social standards.

You are stimulated by art, poetry, music, drama, philosophy, and science. You identify with the entire world about you, rather than just the society in which you live. Other ages and other cultures influence your thinking and add stimulus to your creative ability. You reach out wide and high, and though your two feet may not always be firmly on the earth, it was Shakespeare who said, "We are such stuff as dreams are made on." You who have chosen the squiggle form as the first choice need only remind yourself to put the dream into action.

Evaluating Your Motivation Symbols

On the following pages you will find the sequence of motivation symbols in the order of your original selection. Be sure that your first and second choices are also indicated in your handwriting sample. If they are not, then you must select, in order of frequency, the symbols that appear in writing as the true evaluation.

LOVE SYMBOL

○ □ △ ⚡ You are most motivated by love and the desire to share your pleasures with another or others. You next seek to secure this love by building a foundation of home, family, and friends and will direct most of your energies toward preserving it. You do not wish anything to interfere or disturb the lifestyle you have patterned for yourself and you feel threatened by changes. You are happy with your immediate surroundings and with people familiar in this setting. Ambition is limited to striving for the security of love and family. You are a conservative who stays close to the middle of the road. You accept yourself as an integral part of the society, working for it rather than obstructing it. You are most happy in the role of mate, parent, and member of the community.

○ □ ⚡ △ You, also, are most motivated by love and the desire to share pleasures. The need for security is second only to wanting love and to being loved. These feelings are aesthetic and highly principled, as you are inclined to view basic urges and drives as crude and callous. You are not goal oriented nor abitious in worldly gain, except to ensure the comfort of family and home

living. You avoid a fight and it is most painful when you are con-
fronted with such a situation. You are not competitive, for your nature
is one of friendliness rather than challenge. You will lend your interest, time, and effort as a member of a community group to work
toward improved standards for all. Having the quality of compassion
you will not hurt another and will not like being a witness to another's
injury. Having the capacity for pleasure, with an added touch of
imagination, you make many people very happy.

○ △ □ ⚡ When the triangle (sex symbol) immediately
follows the circle (love symbol) it indicates that
love is the strong motivation behind your sexual expression and drive
for personal achievement. Love gives impetus to your determination
to succeed in the things you undertake. The combination of circular
and triangular shapes in the same handwriting is rare. You have two
extremes to your nature. One is taking the time to be playful, loving,
and compassionate and enjoying the pleasure of being with people.
The other is an aggressive drive to get ahead without the interference
of emotional feelings to slow you down. However, these two extremes
ultimately come together. Though your ambition may sometimes
conceal how you feel inwardly, you always involve others in both your
pleasures and successes. You are a realist with both feet on the ground,
preferring to accept and move on solid and sound ideas, rather than
reach for the unreachable.

○ △ ⚡ □ You are most motivated by the desire for love,
which is also the major factor behind your sexual
expression and drive for accomplishment. You have a touch of ro-
manticism and momentary flights into fantasy. This does not disturb
your balance or pace, but adds excitement and novelty to the goals
you have already set out to achieve. You are least concerned with
financial security or the kind of security measured by social standards.
You view this as a type of confinement rather than a source of protec-
tion and resist being bound to structures. The home may be your
castle, but the house is not. The home to you is yourself and the people
whom you allow to visit with you on an intimate basis. You are not
afraid to face problems and try to resolve them. You put all personal
freedoms before safety of self and property. For you, the only security
is the freedom to express your feelings and abilities.

○ ⚵ □ △   You are a romantic idealist. You will search for a profound love with another individual, one which you look for to satisfy every emotion and desire. This search dominates most of your thinking, time, and emotional energy. You are extremely imaginative and will unconsciously invent an image of another which is unreal. This results in a temporary disillusion and disappointment until you make a transfer to another person which is equally unreal.

You appreciate beauty and creativity and identify yourself with the aesthetic values of the culture. Anything esoteric is appealing, for you are excited and stimulated by new discoveries and the search for knowledge beyond the present understanding of mankind. Wealth and social success are of little concern to you. You are interested in attaining loftier goals to satisfy your abundant emotional needs. Your thinking is not geared to meeting the struggle and competition which exist in the business world and you are bored and impatient with following systems. If you are to be a success in the world in an artistic endeavor, you should have an agent to represent you so that you can be free from outside harassment.

○ ⚵ △ □   The preceding sequence applies to you except that you are more aggressive in your search for love and more ambitious in finding outlets for your creative abilities. You will also stand up to other people who threaten your ideals and principles and will fight for the right to express yourself in your own way. You have the ability to provide spiritual leadership without the quest for power, for you are motivated by the desire to explore the greater possibilities and rewards of love.

SECURITY SYMBOL ▢

□ ○ △ ⚵   The most important thing in your life is for you to feel safe and secure. When you reach for something, you first make sure you are able to grasp and hold onto it, otherwise you will not reach for it at all. Your home is your most valuable possession and everything contained in it. Whatever pleasures you might enjoy on the outside, you will sacrifice if they jeopardize the stability and security of your home and family life. Your view of love is that it belongs within the family unit, and even if it is lacking there, you are not happy compensating for it elsewhere. You are in step with the culture and the society and enjoy the comforts of friends and family. Being a peace-loving individual you abhor violence and corruption. Though you do not conceive of far-range purposes, you are most concerned with a well-structured and safe society and will apply your efforts in this direction both in your home and community.

You are a builder, building long and lasting friendships and maintaining family ties. You can be counted on to be reasonable and logical in living situations, and will compromise in order to satisfy others as well as yourself. Your thought and action are based on what you believe is practical. You rarely act on emotion and desire alone and quite frequently you feel that you live a dull existence. You may feel unstimulating and unimaginative, but many people find in you a solid and trustworthy individual.

□ ○ ♄ △ Again, the preceding sequence also fits you, with these few changes. You are more imaginative and romantic and will tend to glamourize your love interests and home situation so that they become the source of your pleasure as well as satisfying your need for security. You are even less ambitious and competitive and will not struggle for fame or worldly gain beyond what you require for comfortable living. You enjoy simple pleasures and find that they are easily accessible to you. You are not frustrated if you are unable to attain luxuries, and find that you can adjust to living without them. Your greatest concern is to maintain a safe and happy home.

□ △ ○ ♄ This is a dynamic sequence for you, the security-motivated individual. You take aggressive action to ensure the security of you and your family, and are willing to compete and fight for it. You are intelligent, and your approach to problems is both perceptive and logical. Therefore, you act first on reason rather than emotion, making you more often a winner than a loser.

Like a builder, you apply your energy to constructive purposes to help provide a good life-style for you and your family.

You believe in authority and discipline in both the home and in business, and are not easily swayed by tears or hard-luck stories. For you all things have a calculable worth and meaning, and you are intent upon learning what they are. People view you as cold and impersonal, with little romance to your nature. You haven't taken much time to dream and fantasize, to play for play's sake or to give love freely. Purpose and reason guide your emotional feelings. Love and play are extravagant luxuries which interfere with your objectives.

□ △ ⚸ ○　You are in most ways similar to the preceding description, as the first two symbols dominate and indicate the same major motivation. You, however, are more imaginative and will add a touch of creative thought to the things you make and do. You use your imagination to develop plans and ideas further, rather than for play and romance, for you respond to challenges and enjoy solving problems. You are a serious-minded individual most intent upon keeping your emotions under control, your thinking organized, and your ability to produce on a high level. You do not look to have your ego fed by others, but seek security and self-actualization from your own accomplishments. You are motivated to keep all things in place and in order, and though you may not enjoy a great deal of lighthearted fun and pleasure from close relationships with other people, you gain great satisfaction from personal achievement.

□ ⚸ ○ △　You are not an easy person to understand or to live with, for there are two strongly opposing factors which motivate you. You respond first to practical reasoning and logic, intent upon gaining the important essentials to lead an orderly life. Your first reaction to your surroundings is to fit into them and you view the environment with a positive attitude of mutual exchange. This offers you the feeling of being secure and you are prompted to give as well as take for the advantage of this security. Your primary need is to feel that your ideas and actions have a solid foundation, and that they will not crumble as they encounter the storms of life.

You are next motivated by an intense desire to explore the unknown, to be able to stretch your imagination beyond what is practical and reasonable. An inner voice tells you there is more to build in life than an organized pattern of social living, and you, the solid, practical mind, reach for the unreachable and envision the invisible. You are constantly in conflict between acting from a point of practicality and one which is unrealistic. You are a builder, but you are often building castles in the air, and when you come down from them to your actual abode, you find it dull and unstimulating. The urge for an exciting and romantic life is strong, but you will not sacrifice it for what you have that is real, no matter how you protest or how unsatisfying that measure of reality is. You will not let go of it.

Routine and sameness create great frustration, and you rebel against the lack of change in your life. Yet you are not sufficiently aggressive to make your station in life more enchanting, for you will not compete on the levels set up by society. Recognition from friends and family and your own personal creative achievements offer some measure of satisfaction. Religious and philosophical pursuits are likely avenues for your creative expression.

☐ ⚹ △ ○ Frank Lloyd Wright was an architect with imagination and intense drive. You are also a builder, though you may be concerned with building things other than those of brick and wood. Your ideas are constructed on a solid base, and though imagination may sweep you away on wild tangents, your ability to perceive a problem allows for using imaginative thought to a practical end. You are not overly aggressive, but have sufficient initiative to put some of your plans into action, which makes you a candidate for contributing in a real and functioning way to society and your own life. It takes you awhile to reach a particular goal, because you often indulge in fantasy and daydreaming which slow you down.

You don't have much fun, in the frivolous sense, for you are too serious-minded in your objectives to secure home and family and to emerge as a self-actualized individual. You aren't interested in developing close relationships with other people, as they are not your source of pleasure, though you are able to relate without getting emotionally involved. Your aesthetic values are high, and the desire to bring a balance of the real world and your dreams into your living situation is your ultimate goal.

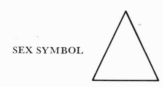

SEX SYMBOL

△ ○ □ ⚷ It would be an oversimplification to state that you are most motivated by sex, since the triangle is represented as the tool for aggressive energy which may find many outlets for expression. You are a self-motivated individual with an abundant supply of energy which seeks constantly to release itself. People are extremely important to you. You have a greater need to express love than to receive it, and so in your associations with others you become more the giver than the taker. You do not hesitate to take an action and will not just wait around for somebody else to make a move or to come up with an idea—you're generally there first.

You enjoy competition and challenges, especially those involved in selling yourself to other people, and you are not easily discouraged. Having a quick mind and keen perception gives you a strong advantage in these pursuits. You frequently act on impulse and intuition, taking chances and endangering your security. Long and drawn-out projects begin to bore you, as you are anxious to move on to new things. Impatient with vague probabilities and idealistic philosophies, you like to deal with concrete realities and get to the heart of things.

It is uncommon to find triangles and circles in the same handwriting. This combination makes it difficult for the people who play an important part in your life. You are aggressive in play and in love, but your attitude and behavior toward others will often change from warm and loving to hostile and intolerant. This leaves them feeling confused and insecure in their relationship with you. You have the capacity to be understanding and compassionate, but this is often subdued by your impatient urge to push ahead.

You are geared for action, direct in your approach, basic in your needs and desires, and intent upon satisfying them. You do not sublimate the things you want or seek vicarious pleasures. You want the real thing and you want it quickly.

△ ○ ⚷ □ The only variable in this sequence from the preceding one is that your energies are even more dynamic, because they are fed with greater imagination. You will invent and create different approaches to achieve the things you want. Security is of least importance to you, in the social living sense, and you are readily bored with home activities. Attending to routine chores is cumbersome and you avoid them. Though playful, you are easily antagonized. You become explosive when provoked and have great difficulty in controlling your temper. After the storm, you forgive easily, and can become just as passionate in your love as in your hate.

You are a person of dynamic energy, sensuality, and keen thinking. A disciple of the pleasure principle, you have the capacity really to enjoy life.

△ □ ○ ♃   You will find that by comparison with the first two triangle-dominated sequences you are not quite so pleasure bound, though a much easier person to live with. Your aggressive energy looks for constructive outlets which depend more upon your own abilities than being emotionally fed by others. You possess the kind of mind which has the power to perceive a situation quickly. Once perceived, you can patiently evaluate with reason and logic and follow through with the necessary steps to resolve it. You do not allow your emotions to interfere with your reason. You act on knowledge rather than on what you feel.

You have a good mind plus good manual ability, allowing you to work out your own ideas independently. You have clear thoughts about what you want and take direct steps toward achieving objectives. Though not particularly artistic or creative, you will explore and persevere until you have successfully completed a project. A realist, with both feet on the ground, you are much too busy to fantasize and daydream.

△ □ ♃ ○   Your motivation evaluation is the same as those in the preceding sequence, except that you are able to experience more creative thought. You will occasionally find the time to look for romance and idealism in the things you do and take pride in efforts where you have contributed your own imaginative abilities. You are serious-minded and do not take much time out for fun. Your idea of a good time is to attack a problem or a project and work it out successfully. You do not devote much time or effort to developing further the personal relationships you have, nor are you particularly understanding of or giving to the emotional needs of others. You have somewhat alienated the child in you and, therefore, have difficulty in relating to the child in another person. To perceive and then to perform is your goal.

△ ⚡ ○ □   You are a highly individualistic personality. Your power of imagination and high aggressive energy give you unlimited scope for expression. You generate a great amount of mental activity which searches for creative outlets. You are not bound to conventionalism, tradition, and social mores, but seek out the universal order and nature of things. Uninvolved with the immediate environment of home, friends, establishment, your true motive is to reach the more profound truths existing beyond the comprehension of society's group living. Your behavior is mostly dominated by an intense urge to move ahead in gaining new knowledge and insight.

Alone in thought a good deal of the time, even though you may physically be in the company of other people, you find you are most productive and creative when in seclusion. You are stimulated both by fact and fantasy and will use this combination to express yourself artistically. It is difficult for you to find others who move on a similar plane. You disdain shallowness and superficial attitudes. Gossip and small talk bore you, therefore, your friends are select and few.

Your view of security is in terms of universal survival rather than the preservation of any one body or culture. Your goal is to identify with the entire universe and in your lifetime to contribute to it.

△ ⚡ □ ○   You, like those in the preceding sequence, are an energetic and creative person, highly individualistic in your expression. Most of the above description applies also to you, but with a few important differences. You are more conscious of a need to feel secure in your actual living situation. Because of this you are more inclined to conform to the demands of society in order to preserve and continue your life-style and to enjoy some of the comforts provided.

The demands you make upon yourself are great. You tax yourself both physically and mentally, leaving little energy for fun and games.

Though you have a penetrating mind, it is difficult for others to penetrate your surface and really get to know you because you resist becoming emotionally involved on a person-to-person basis. You require more compassion and understanding from others than you are able to give to them, but you are well equipped to give something of value to a great many people, though the giving is nonpersonally inspired. You do not find a satisfying love in one human being.

IMAGINATION SYMBOL

You are sensitive and idealistic, always looking for beauty and romance even in the most simple and basic functions of life. You search for a pure and aesthetic love, one that transcends the urge to satisfy basic needs. Though often alone in a higher atmosphere of thought, you need the warmth and security of being with people. Friends are often a disappointment to you, as they seldom live up to the qualities you originally attribute to them. When offended or hurt, you will temporarily withdraw, but you will rarely act with hostility against anyone. You will find a refuge in some artistic, philosophical, or spiritual expression.

Ambition is not your motivation. You are more a thinker than an action person, with no powerful drive for worldly success. You reach for the unknown and find pleasure in dreams and fantasy. People are very important to you. You are warm and responsive to those who accept you as an individual and who recognize the creative things you do. Though you may never blaze a trail to fame, you can offer a great deal of stimulating pleasure to yourself and others who walk along with you.

Imaginative, loving, and playful, you can become aggressive if your pleasures are threatened. You are also sensitive and idealistic, and will defend your principles even if your security is in danger, for you measure your security in terms of freedom to express yourself. You are drawn to the esoteric, reaching for higher levels of thought and more profound emotional feelings.

Uncomfortable in tight quarters, you need expansive room to move about in, so that you do not feel boxed in. You want to think, feel, and act without restriction. You rebel against imposed discipline, systems, and standardized procedures. The greatest pleasure you experience is in discovery, and your love for other human beings makes you want to share it with them.

You are in many ways similar to those in the first imagination-dominated sequence, but your initiative to act on your feelings and ideals makes an important difference.

⚷ □ ○ △   You are both a dreamer and a realist, escaping into the broad realms of your imagination and then pulling yourself back into the safer confines of a real world. Though you have lofty thoughts and tend to be carried away by vivid impressions fused together by your imagination, you are also very much aware of your true body existence and its environment. Your openness to new ideas and willingness to see and accept change can work positively in your developing an inherent ability to adjust to any situation or change. This quality also gives you greater satisfaction of home and adds charm to your daily living.

Since your need for security is also very strong, you manage to keep both feet on the ground consistently enough to function as a member of the social environment. Home is important, but you need variety and change to feed your stronger motivational need. You should draw upon your creative talent to lend nuance and stimulation even to your home situation. You are a natural builder who can put pieces together and come out with a whole. You have the patience to use logic and reason, and will do so when you are not flying on the wings of fantasy. Then you are able to apply your own personal creative touches to whatever purpose, and follow it through with diligence.

You are neither violent nor hostile. Your talents seek expression in ways that will please not only yourself, but also others.

⚷ □ △ ○   Your motivation evaluation is the same as those in the preceding sequence. You may accept the entire description with the exception of the last paragraph. You can become hostile and foster resentment, especially when you are interrupted or held back from your pursuits. You are more involved with self than with other people, intent upon gaining personal satisfactions rather than sharing them. Personal relationships take a back seat to your other interests. Even family ties are more a means of securing your need for home stability than for exchanging a personal love. You have an even greater ability to adjust to situations since you are less influenced by other people and emotional attachments to them.

� △ ○ ☐ You are truly a dynamic individual, possessing all the qualities for success and leadership. You have a mind that is never at rest, but is operating in high gear all the time, generating new thoughts and images. You explore vague possibilities, bringing them into focus with keen comprehension and then succeeding to produce solid ideas. You assimilate knowledge and understand abstract concepts without working at it too hard or too long, expecting others to follow through with the details of your planned projects as you become bored with minor procedures. Your objective is mentally to create and solve; the actual carrying out is elementary and can be handled by the nonthinkers.

You enjoy challenges; in fact, they are a source of stimulation and pleasure. You search for a variety of areas to discharge your mental energies which are continuously building up as they are being released. Receptive to new ideas, you are still too sharp-minded to become a pawn for any way-out philosophies or movements which you believe do not conform to an intelligent order.

In relationships, people either envy you or are in awe of you. You frequently present a threat to their feelings of their own self-image. You are far from the ideal companion or mate, for you have spent little time developing socially, and are intolerant of the weaknesses of others. You do have need for companionship, consciously or unconsciously seeking alliances with those reflecting your characteristics. Because you are so highly individualistic, you rarely encounter satisfying company. The price you pay for your dynamics is loneliness.

You are least motivated by the desire for security. With all your serious thinking, you would like to be able to relax with people, be playful, and enjoy more simple pleasures. You have sufficient awareness and liking for other people to use your imagination and intelligence to enjoy them more.

⚿ △ ☐ ○   You are the same dynamic individual as the one described in the preceding sequence, with similar drives and motives. However, you are even less motivated to develop strong relationships and have little compassion and patience with others. You resist social amenities and do not consider yourself part of the group or institution. Not much of your free time is devoted to party or play, and even humor must be sprinkled with provocative thought to be appealing. People generally regard you either as extremely stimulating, or boringly eccentric.

Your need for companionship is minor. You are primarily self-oriented, self-motivated, and independent. You have powerful positive forces to distinguish yourself by contributing to something more and different to the world, though not to any one individual.

The motivation symbols and their respective sequences are only valid when you confirm them by their order of frequency in your handwriting sample. To ensure accuracy, follow this procedure:

1. The written sample may be done with pen or pencil, but it should be an implement you are accustomed to using. Approximately ten lines will be ample. It must be prepared with a salutation, a message, a closing, and a full signature, preferably written to someone you know fairly well. Write on an 8½″ x 11″ unlined sheet of paper, in a comfortable position and at a time when you will be undisturbed. This sample will be used also for later self-evaluation, so do not destroy it.

2. For your motivation evaluation you need only work with the first four words of the letter message. Repeat only these four words on another sheet of paper so that you don't disturb the original sample. You will have no trouble determining the dominant symbols that appear in your letter forms, nor those that come after, as long as you follow the procedure outlined. Here are examples for scoring yourself.

I truly love you

DOMINANT LOVE SYMBOL   ○ ☐ ⚿ △

All the letter forms and connecting strokes reflect a circular movement except the *r* in the word "truly" and the two *o* extensions which are square. The third form which appears is part of the imagination squiggle in the beginning swing of the *I* and the *l* in the word "love." The triangle is not evidenced at all and, therefore, is placed last in the sequence.

Your home is lovely

DOMINANT SECURITY SYMBOL   □ △ ○ ⚡

The most frequent shape here is the square as seen in the capital *Y* and most of the middle-zone letters. The triangle appears next in frequency in the word "is" and the *v* in the word "lovely," as well as the middle part of the ending *y*. The *o*'s are too narrow to be considered as circles, but the *e*'s are acceptable as circular movements. There are no additions or variations, therefore, the imagination symbol is placed last in the sequence.

I must see you!

DOMINANT SEX SYMBOL   △ ⚡ ○ □

There can be no question about the triangular movements in this sample, as they are apparent in most of the writing pattern. The symbol for imagination, which also includes inventiveness, is demonstrated by the unique *I,* the way the *t* bar crosses and moves to the *s* and the imaginative forming of the exclamation mark. The circle is seen in the *s* curve and in the movement leading to the exclamation mark. No square shapes are visible.

I wish for everything

DOMINANT IMAGINATION SYMBOL   ⚡ ○ □ △

The high reach of the upper letters, the added swing and variation to the forms, and the distinguishing strokes are the most salient characteristics of this writing. Next you must score the love symbol, since most of the movements have a circular motion. The square follows as seen in the formation of the *r*'s. There are no points or triangular shapes; therefore, the sex symbol is scored last.

When you have difficulty in deciding whether a letter is more round, more square, or more triangular, trust your own judgment. It's the best one you have to go on. Letters are imaginative and creative when they add something new or are expressed uniquely without destroying or misrepresenting the true nature of the letter.

Indicate here the original selection of symbols you made by choice.

Original Choice Sequence _____

Now record below the symbols which occurred in your handwriting sample by order of frequency.

Handwriting Symbol Sequence _____

The symbol sequence found in your handwriting is your true motivation evaluation. You may conclude that you are quite aware of yourself and have a pretty good idea of who you are if the two sequences are identical.

2.

the emotional you

All of us have preconceived notions about ourselves. We think we know what our attitudes, ideas, abilities, and feelings are, and also have an impression of how we project ourselves to others. Our behavior is largely influenced by what we think of ourselves and what we believe others think of us.

In order to determine whether or not your self-conception is in accord with facets of your personality uncovered through your handwriting, it is important that you complete the following questionnaire to the best of your ability. Be sure to do this before you read the chapter so your answers are not influenced by anything other than what you believe is true about yourself.

You will have an opportunity to compare your own self-evaluation with the knowledge of yourself discovered through the handwriting sample. The objective is to open up doors to some of your inner chambers which have never been opened before. With a little oiling at the hinges of those unyielding places, it won't be too difficult. If you hear a few squeaks, don't be upset; it's a sign that these barriers can be moved so you can get through.

There are some things you may never have questioned yourself about and actually cannot answer. If this is so, check the question mark.

Yes	No	?	
——	——	——	1. Do you like people and enjoy being with them most of the time?
——	——	——	2. Are you a pushover for a hard-luck story?
——	——	——	3. Do you lean heavily on others for love and affection?
——	——	——	4. Are you reserved and objective with people, taking the time to know them well before allowing yourself to become emotionally involved?
——	——	——	5. Are you a loner, preferring your own company to that of others?
——	——	——	6. Are you a loner because you feel uncomfortable with people?
——	——	——	7. Are you unable to relate to anyone at all?
——	——	——	8. Do you experience constantly changing moods, reacting warmly to people sometimes and feeling cold toward them at other times?
——	——	——	9. Are you a loner, but one who knows how to play the social game and does it when you feel it necessary?
——	——	——	10. Are you completely confused about your feelings for people, not sure whether you want friends or not?

If you are unable to answer some of these questions, after completing this chapter you will be quite illuminated.

All parts of your personality are related, each dependent upon its interaction with all the others. For example, your behavior cannot be judged without understanding the way you think. The way you think is influenced by the way you feel emotionally and physically. Your emotions guide your attitudes about yourself and the society. All these parts must be looked at separately and then together in order to understand you—a total person.

Your emotions are governed by some basic factors. At birth you have already inherited some emotional characteristics, which then begin to develop through a natural process of growth. Your particular experiences and surroundings further influence your emotional development. Since you have no control over the legacy of traits left you by your ancestors, it is more fruitful to find how these traits developed from infancy on up. In searching for answers, the intention is not to judge yourself, but only to understand why you feel the way you do today. For example, if as a child you suffered periods of illness which frightened you and caused you to need someone near most of the time, you might continue to have a fear of being alone as an adult, even though illness may no longer be a problem. If you were a robust child venturing into dangerous situations—swimming alone, getting into fights, exploring haunted houses, and asserting a measure of independence—then you established a pattern which made you an emotionally secure adult.

Intelligence can influence emotional growth. The greater your potential is for learning, the broader is your scope of areas in which to feel and respond. As a small child, you feel sadness for the bird with a broken wing, only because you know the bird can no longer fly. As a farmer you worry about the drought, as a pilot you fear an electrical storm, as a parent you are concerned about the drug problem, and the more you know about things the more you are able to have truer feelings about them.

Your understanding of the kinds of feelings you had as a child is your most useful tool in being able to see and accept yourself as an adult. Your feelings for other people will also grow and be more rewarding as you begin to consider the child operating in them. This gaining insight of human behavior is an invaluable asset. It does not mean that a person with limited scope and understanding does not have the capacity for intense emotion. Unchanneled emotions often burst forth with even greater energy, but their lack of control and direction creates trauma and short-term satisfaction.

FIND THE DIRECTION OF YOUR EMOTIONS

Your emotional attitude toward yourself in relation with other people is most strongly reflected in your handwriting slant. Find the slant which most closely approximates your own, then you may read the corresponding description of your emotional reactions on the following pages:

FORWARD (a)   *I am fond of you.*

FORWARD (b)

I am in love with you.

FORWARD (c)

I need you desperately

UPRIGHT   *I find you amusing.*

BACKWARD (a)   *I'd like to be alone*

BACKWARD (b)

I can't identify with anyone

BACKWARD (c)

I can't stand to be with people.

In some individual handwritings, two different slants exist in the same word or line of writing, as in the examples listed below:

FORWARD AND UPRIGHT

Sometimes I like to be by myself.

UPRIGHT AND BACKWARD

I don't know what I want.

FORWARD AND BACKWARD

Only I know what is real!

At Harvard University Psychology Clinic, studies were conducted by two psychologists, Gordon Allport and Philip Vernon, to throw light on whether all movements are consistent with one another. Their findings indicated a relationship and organized pattern of all expressive movements and characteristics, attitudes and values of the inner personality. My own research corroborates this view. When your physical gestures move forward, your emotional feelings lean in the same direction—from the self to other people. To draw an analogy, you might observe a person speaking to you. If he leans forward, extending his hands in an open gesture, he is offering something of himself to you. This is also true of a handwritten letter of communication. The forward slant is saying that the writer is reaching out to you in a personal way.

Forward. The degree to which your writing slants forward is the degree to which you will extend your personal emotions to others.

(a) You are aware of yourself in relation to other people and cognizant of the effect they have upon your life. You enjoy friendships and social situations and are comfortable in them. You are very much in control of your emotional feeling toward others, and can pull out of a relationship without consuming too much pain or time.

(b) You respond very quickly to people, wanting to get to know them and share feelings and thoughts. You are a pushover for a hard-luck story, often acting with your heart instead of your head. Being compassionate, you forgive easily though you may have suffered personal hurts. You fall in love frequently, and when you get burned you do the same thing all over again.

(c) Your need for love and affection is so intense that you become very dependent emotionally upon the people who are close to you. Desiring to be near them physically and mentally, you tend to stifle them by expecting that they return the same intensity of feelings in a demonstrative way. When rejected, you will become melancholy and morose and indulge in self-pity. Feeding this emotional behavior is an underlying insecurity about your worthiness and ability to maintain relationships.

Upright. You take a neutral position in your attitudes toward people, meeting them with objectivity and reserve. You guard against any emotional involvement until you have had the opportunity really to get to know someone, and even then you are able to see his faults and virtues with clear vision. You think first and then allow yourself to feel or not to feel, depending upon your judgment of the person and the situation. You stand in the comfortable position of having the emotional control to select or reject objects of affection. Of course, you sacrifice the pleasure of spontaneous feelings.

Backward. Many graphologists prefer not to use the term "backward" because of its implication in regard to personality. However, because it is directly opposite to the forward-writing movement, it best describes the slant referred to. Left-handedness is not a cause for backward movement in writing, for many left-handed writers move upright and forward. Even with the disadvantage of not having corrected the turned-under position of the hand in developing writing habits, the emotionally responsive personality will seek the forward direction, though the speed of writing will be slower.

(a) If your handwriting slant is backward, it indicates that you draw away from people. You do not seek them out, and when they approach, you move back, putting distance between you. You prefer to be alone, work alone, and think alone. It is difficult for anyone to reach you on a personal level, for you ward off communicating with others. You have sufficient emotional control to conceal this attitude from family, friends, and associates; however, you cannot control the discomfort and uneasiness you feel in social company. No matter what impression you may convey, you are truly a loner.

(b) The preceding description also applies to you, but to a much greater degree. It is actually painful for you to be exposed to social situations and you avoid them whenever possible. You are not too successful in hiding your feelings, as you literally back off from people as they are approaching and are insensitive to them. It is unlikely that you have ever developed rapport or a line of communication with family, and certainly not parents, as you have always resisted the authority of a social structure. This continued resistance prevented you from reaching adequate levels of mutual exchange of thoughts and feelings.

You do not recognize or appreciate the efforts of other people in your behalf, and do not move to give something of yourself to them. You see yourself as an entity separate and apart from anyone else, without awareness or concern for the interdependency of all human beings. Therefore, you do not feel a responsibility to the world in which you live.

(c) This slant indicates an extremely withdrawn individual. You are very involved with only your particular needs and quite desperate in the desire to satisfy them. They are bizarre and unrealistic, but you have moved so far away from the actual living environment that these needs are in keeping with your sense of reality. You are extremely emotional and feeling, though it is not extended to or exchanged with other people. Society's principles and laws do not apply to you, and, if your handwriting indicates aggressive qualities, you will actively defy them.

If you lean back much farther, you will completely lose your balance and fall flat on your back.

Forward and Upright. This combination is not uncommon, providing the upright does not appear with the extreme forward (c) slant. If your slant is upright with forward (a), you are fairly consistent in emotional response to people, sometimes a little more reactive, and at other times a trifle more reserved. In either state you are pretty much in control of your feelings, enjoying each mood as it comes upon you.

If the upright appears with forward (b), you are subject to tense and changing feelings. For you and those with whom you are involved, this creates confusion and lack of confidence in the relationship, since neither you nor they can depend upon your emotional behavior from time to time. On one occasion you are warm and responsive to someone, and on another, cool and unemotive to the same person. The intervals between may be as brief as a week, a day, or an hour. Some people accept you as you are, but many are hurt and offended by the shift to an impersonal you. You experience strain and exhaustion because of these emotional jumps over which you have little control, and require greater understanding from friends and family.

If the upright appears with forward (c), you are in need of emotional guidance from a professional source. This extreme movement from a reserved and impersonal emotional behavior to an expression of desperation for love and affection is too great a jump not to have some damaging effect. Here is an example of the extreme change in hand movement, which also reflects the extreme change in emotional feelings:

I don't care, but I do lose you.

One of the problems you encounter is the embarrassment at having exposed those innermost feelings and emotional vulnerability. Recognizing this aspect of your nature as a weakness, you then pull back to a position of control. You bound forward and backward like a rubber ball, straining your energy which has an effect upon your total functioning.

Upright and Backward. If your slant is upward and backward (a) you are very discerning, with the ability to size up other people. You calculate them as you would a problem and will accept them as friends if they fit into your way of life and meet the standards you have set. You enjoy social situations on a cool and impersonal level, knowing how to play the game, but more frequently desiring not to. Your emotional detachment from most situations allows you to act with reason and judgment, and in this respect you are a valuable friend, though not a close one.

The upright with backward (b) shows that you are engaged in a struggle to hold onto reality but encounter forces pulling you back into a world of introspection. You want to identify on some levels with other people, but also to shut them out from other areas where you can live in isolation. When you do relate to people it is primarily for the purpose of keeping contact with the world. You are not sensitive to them or emotionally involved. There exists the danger that the periods of withdrawing may become more comfortable and enjoyable than the pleasures derived from interacting with the real world. The handwriting will begin to show fewer upright movements and more backward ones.

The upright and backward (c) combination indicates that you require professional guidance to resolve your emotional problems. Periods of withdrawal are so extreme and deep that the transition back to accepting your role in the society must throw you emotionally off balance. When you lean so far backward and then almost immediately stand up straight, without making the in-between movements, there is a shake-up of your equilibrium. Note the jump in action in this sample:

Whatever you decide, I still need time to make my decision.

If you can gradually accelerate all your movements toward the neutral zone, your tensions will be reduced.

Forward and Backward.   This combination shows a complete reversal of direction and muscle action within the same phrase of writing. A tremendous strain occurs in moving from one pole to the other, affecting you emotionally and physically, and throwing off your balance, rhythm, and coordination.

Forward (c) with backward (c) is extremely rare. Adolf Hitler's handwriting came close to it. This combined movement is even difficult to simulate, but it would appear like this:

You are incapable of doing

This is the movement of a fractured personality, capable of extreme dualism. The emotional state changes drastically from total withdrawal from people to a hungry yearning and need to be close to them. In either state, the personality is completely involved with itself, making demands but unable to give to others. The disposition is erratic and explosive. With consideration of other characteristics in the handwriting, this person can be very dangerous to himself and others.

All combinations of backward and forward slant in the same writing sample indicate emotional turmoil and stress. The degree to which the writing moves backward and then forward determines how seriously the emotional balance is affected. Picture yourself leaning backward and forward while walking. The action will be awkward and clumsy, you may stumble or trip, becoming confused about where you are going and not making much headway in getting there. The same thing occurs with emotional expression when guiding the writing implement across a sheet of paper.

If your handwriting sample shows a combined slant that is not described here, take the individual explanations for each and by evaluating them together you will find your emotional evaluation.

Now go back to the questionnaire on page 44 and compare the original thoughts you had about yourself with what you have discovered in your handwriting. How well do you know your own emotional reactions to people?

Emotional Slant _____

3.

the physical you

Again, fill out this questionnaire before you read the rest of the chapter.

Yes   No   ?

___   ___   ___   1. Do you move quickly?

___   ___   ___   2. Are your movements evenly paced and balanced?

___   ___   ___   3. Do you choose the fastest, shortest direction to arrive at your destination?

___   ___   ___   4. Are you always looking for shortcuts?

___   ___   ___   5. Do you think before you act?

___   ___   ___   6. Do you grasp firmly and move with confidence?

___   ___   ___   7. Do you frequently trip and stumble?

___   ___   ___   8. Are you almost always fired with physical energy and drive?

___   ___   ___   9. Do you often run out of steam and feel fatigue easily?

Yes	No	?	
——	——	——	10. Do you experience extreme changes from feeling very energetic to periods of dull laziness?
——	——	——	11. Are you determined to get where you're going without being sidetracked?
——	——	——	12. Do you become disturbed and irritable when your physical activity is restricted?
——	——	——	13. Do you always operate in high gear, unable to relax even when you have the time?
——	——	——	14. Are you frequently confused about where you are and where you are going?
——	——	——	15. Do you often do things with a feeling that it isn't what you want to do at all?
——	——	——	16. Are you unhappy with your pace of action, knowing it is not up to your capabilities?

You will find many answers on the following pages.

There is so much interplay between physical and mental energy that each one cannot be measured independently. A physical act relies as much upon thought, desire, and will as it does upon the body's ability to carry it out. An exhausted swimmer will manage to swim that extra length to win the race, and in an emergency we have all been able to summon unusual strength and endurance. The opposite is also true, for emotions can weaken physical acts which the body is normally capable of performing. A virile man can become impotent with an undesirable woman, an A student fail an examination under pressure, and an artist may perform poorly when he is in distress. You have been a witness to many such situations. When you observe someone about to perform an act of skill or strength, you will note the few moments he takes to prepare himself for the action.

Your physical needs and desires are constantly adjusted to your thinking, and certainly your thinking is influenced by physical needs. Which has greater control—mind over body or body over mind? Fortunately, the vast majority of people are able to exert mind over body. Most individuals are able to adjust their thinking to changing conditions because of their will to survive. This is the mind instructing the body to obey its direction.

In each person there is a varying supply of physical energy which seeks to be released. Your mind directs the flow of this energy, selecting ways in which it can be liberated. This is what distinguishes you as one physical person from another.

In this chapter you will learn how your physical energy is put to use and how it is revealed in the handwriting. You will have the opportunity to note and record your own physical characteristics.

Nobody has to teach the infant to reach out with his hand and grasp, nor to creep or crawl. This occurs as a natural process of growth. The infant may respond more rapidly when a fanciful object is placed in front of him, or crawling may be retarded if the infant is kept lying on his back and is unable to turn over. The urge to use all parts of your body is inherent. Whether or not you use them to the intended capacity during each stage of growing up depends greatly upon how much you are motivated and what stumbling blocks are put in your path. Motivating factors for action mindedness include sensation and pleasure, recognition, approval, and general reinforcement of basic security needs. Major stumbling blocks are improper nutrition and rest, inadequate environment for learning experience, and lack of the motivating factors stated above which results in a poor self-image. The ability to overcome any of these weakening conditions indicates a power of will and mind for which there is no explanation other than to conclude that some things are God-given.

The three important considerations in determining the amount of your action mindedness are the speed, force, and direction of your movements. These are discernible in your handwriting.

SPEED

When the infant is finally able to grasp a block in each hand, he bangs them both together in an upward and downward motion rather than from the sides toward the center. When the child goes to school and begins to print, he finds it more difficult to make horizontal strokes than vertical ones. You can prove this, as an adult, by drawing both horizontal and vertical lines with the hand you are not accustomed to using. You will discover that not only are the horizontal lines more difficult to make, but they are also more poorly executed. Therefore, a vertical pattern of writing lends itself to greater speed.

The circular and square-shaped letters slow down writing speed, but the triangular movement is geared to a quick pace.

In order to qualify as quick-moving letters, they must show a smooth line that has no stopping points. Narrow loops require less time than full ones, further increasing speed. If your letter forms show the linear quality as in the sample below, score yourself "Yes" for letter form speed.

lets get to the issue at hand

Letter Form Speed   Yes ____   No ____

Size.   More movement and time are used for writing large than for small writing. A child normally writes much larger than an adult because it requires skill and concentration to reduce the size of letter forms and still maintain their clarity. He doesn't have to be as careful with bigger letters and less time demands are made upon him. Only the upper and lower loops are made modestly because he is afraid to move too far away from the central zone. The size of middle-zone letters taught in most schools is a quarter-inch in height. For the adult script, it is considered large and it will cut down the speed of the writer. If your middle-zone letters are as small or smaller than this sample, you may indicate "Yes" to letter size speed.

small letters help facilitate speed.

Letter Size Speed   Yes ____   No ____

Letter Connections.   Everytime an action is interrupted, more time is expended in starting it up again. When letter forms are disconnected, the speed and fluency of the writing are subject to additional pressure. The pen or pencil stops, lifts up from the paper, and has to be set down again in the right place. If your letters are connected to one another, there is more opportunity for continuous action and faster speed.

Letter connections give steady flow

Letter Connection Speed   Yes ____   No ____

Stroke Simplification. Simplified letter forms require less time and energy to write. By omitting strokes which do not define the letter itself, like those which begin and end a word, and by stripping the letter of all its nonessentials, a great amount of speed can be picked up. A printed form to replace a cursive one is generally done to increase speed. These samples will help you to determine the time economy of your own strokes:

Stroke simplification

Stroke conventionality

Stroke Simplification   Yes ___   No ___

Rhythmic Pattern. The best method of determining the speed of handwriting is by observing the overall rhythmic pattern. Good rhythm is indicated by smooth and unbroken strokes which swing from one letter to the next. There are no corrugations or tiny blotches of ink caused by stopping midway through the stroke. The upward movements of the upper and lower loops will reflect a lighter pressure, as the hand's tensor muscle relaxes with the upward stroke and contracts with the downward one. The spacing between letters and words is consistent, as is the invisible base line of writing.

GOOD RHYTHM

These strokes are smooth and unbroken

POOR RHYTHM

These strokes are awkward and unrhythmical.

Good Rhythm Pattern   Yes ___   No ___

Speed Evaluation

If you answered "Yes" to any one of the criteria of speed in handwriting, your speed of movement is no less than moderate. Two and three of these characteristics qualify your natural speed as fast. If your handwriting shows four or five of these writing traits, you are a racer.

However, no matter how many of these characteristics appear in your writing, if you show a poor rhythmic pattern, your action speed will be slow.

_____ Slow
_____ Moderate
_____ Fast
_____ Racing

FORCE

Force is the power behind the action. The mind directs the amount of force that goes into each action and the body makes the adjustment to its own capability. The mind's direction of force is observable when you shake someone's hand, spank a child, swing a bat, or drive a nail into wood. A forceful person allows himself the freedom to use the energy stored within him. If he is success motivated, he controls where and how it is to be used. Forcefulness is most commonly associated with aggressiveness because it described a power able to drive through barriers and push down obstacles. Success in this competitive society calls for the expenditure of powerful energy. Without this outlay, talents and abilities frequently lie dormant and unrealized.

Force is not always directed into physical areas. A leader commands authority by firmness, self-confidence, and accepting responsibility in giving directives and seeing to it that they are carried out. He does not have to fight on the battlefield. His strength and force are felt by the steadfast and unwavering determination to carry out objectives.

In this segment you will be evaluated by the amount of force you use in your action mindedness. All people sometimes experience feelings of lethargy and at other times are particularly excitable and anxious. Your mood at the time of writing affects this particular characteristic. Thereforce, it is important that you be of normal disposition at the time of your writing. You will find it interesting to note how your handwriting changes as your disposition does.

There are two important factors in determining force. They are pressure and inflexibility. Pressure indicates the amount of power put into the writing. Inflexibility is the steady and unwavering flow of power to each stroke. When strong pressure is found with inflexible forms in the handwriting, it is a sure sign of an energetic, strong-willed, determined, and power-packed personality.

Pressure.   Dark writing is not necessarily evidence of strong pressure. No. 1 or No. 2 pencils and felt-tipped pens will create the impression of heavy writing even when little pressure is exerted. Conversely, a thin point and light-colored ink will give the immediate effect of weak pressure, when there may actually be considerable bearing down with the pen. The paper itself will indicate the amount of pressure used in the handwriting. When the writing implement moves with any amount of force along the paper, an impression is made. By running your fingers over the back of the paper you can feel the indentations. It is also true that pushing down hard with a pen or pencil will cause more ink to flow from the pen and flatten the tip of the pencil, causing a broader and darker stroke. Both these factors are considered in determining writing pressure, though demonstrations of indentations into the paper cannot be shown in the samples here.

The relationship between writing pressure and the forceful personality is easily understood. If you have a firm hold on the writing tool, you will also hold with firmness the things you grasp in life, not allowing them to slip through your fingers. You may also display a firm hold on others, wanting to control them to accomplish your own purposes further, or just out of habit.

A strong grip of the pen before you even begin to write indicates a desire to control the devices you use. This is not without sacrifice, for this need to grip tightly reduces your sensitivity to the object itself, and though you may control it, you haven't much feeling for its true quality. You have undoubtedly observed that the power-driven individual is generally unphilosophical, unaesthetic, and insensitive to the human needs of others. There are exceptions, but when the goal is to chop down the tree, you might never succeed if you begin to consider every branch and leaf. Here are examples of varying pressures.

EXTREME   *Buy up all stock !*

STRONG   *I hired 11 men for the job.*

MODERATE

I'm not sure I can handle this job.

LIGHT

It's too heavy for me to carry.

ALTERNATING

I will, but not at this moment!

Force is not always consistent in the action mindedness of an individual. If your handwriting pressure alternates within the lines of writing of one given sample, you are suffering some emotional disturbance at the time of writing. This quick change in the flow of energy which shows erratic pressure in the writing testifies to a drop and rise of inner strength. This may be the result of a physical problem such as high or low blood pressure, diabetes, malnutrition, poor blood circulation, and other ailments tending to cause fatigue—though mental and emotional energy may be strong.

There are cases of heavy pressure that indicate a lack of force in personality. These cases are particularly observable in young children who hold their pencils tightly between the fingers and very close to the point. The writing fingers are pinched-looking from the tightness of grip and the heavy pressure exerted on the paper. It is not forcefulness which guides their hands in the writing movement, but fear and insecurity. Unsure of their ability to retrace the forms which the teacher has written on the blackboard, they press down on the paper hard, move slowly in an attempt to reproduce the letters properly, and stop frequently to consider the next movement. As the child gains confidence by practice and being able to master the basic principles, the awkward heavy pressure will change.

The same straining pressure in the adult handwriting must be considered differently, as the adult is no longer concerned or afraid of the actual process of writing. Other factors are causing the tension and fear which are manifested in the handwriting. Look closely at the samples below. This pressure is not made by forceful personalities:

CHILD

I don't like writing class.

ADULT

I haven't the patience to write.

The parent and teacher should recognize the existing insecurity of the child and not take a chance that the lack of confidence is just a result of slow adjustment to writing. Too, physical illness may cause this characteristic of writing in both the child and the adult. If the latter is ruled out, it must be concluded that the emotions are working against the personality.

Pressure Evaluation

Your writing pressure is extreme to strong when you can feel the indentations on the reverse sheet of writing and by noting a strong grip on the pen or pencil. Broader strokes will generally appear. Use the samples previously demonstrated to gauge moderate, weak, and alternating pressure. It is easiest to determine insecure pressure.

___ Extreme		___ Weak	
___ Strong		___ Alternating	
___ Moderate		___ Insecure	

We all know that the shortest distance between two points is a straight line. People show this urgency to write their thoughts down fast, without stopping or going around curves and corners whenever possible. Since they avoid time-consuming movements which also take up extra energy, they have more power to apply to their action. A curved ball, thrown with the same amount of force as a straight one, will not have the same impact when reaching its target. Similarly, straight writing strokes give more force to the writing than curved strokes. This is most easily seen in the movement of upper and lower loops, the *d* and *t* stems, and the crossing bar of the *t*.

CURVED STROKES

I'll ask my husband and see what he says.

SQUARE STROKES

I need more facts to make a decision.

INFLEXIBLE STROKES

I mean what I say!

If your letters are more triangular and linear than they are curved and square, you may score yourself "Yes" for inflexibility.

Inflexibility   Yes ___   No ___

Total Force Evaluation

Extreme pressure and inflexibility	___ Dynamic force
Extreme pressure only	___ Strong force
Strong pressure and inflexibility	___ Strong force
Strong pressure only	___ Moderate force
Moderate pressure and inflexibility	___ Moderate force
Moderate pressure only	___ Weak force
All others	___ Nonfunctioning force

Do not be alarmed if you fail to qualify as a force-driven individual. Your particular nature may possess qualities which are sensitive and artistic, and ultimately more rewarding. Force can be compulsive and disturb the emotional system from enjoying more subtle pleasures. Remember, too, that force without direction results in wasted effort or asocial behavior.

DIRECTION

At the beginning of this chapter, the three essentials of action mindedness were stated as speed, force, and direction. The direction of your energies, the goals and objectives toward which you move, is undoubtedly the main determinant of the kind of life you lead. You may possess force and speed in moving, but it is the direction of action which provides real experience in your life.

The forward slant in writing was earlier evaluated in terms of your emotional response to people. The direction toward your goals has been greatly influenced by your experience with people from infancy on up and, therefore, is found in similar writing characteristics. Success, fame, and other worldly ambitions are developed because there is a society which is made up of people. Therefore, you move forward with an awareness that your successes are dependent upon the social structure and the people who move in it.

You look forward to the future, putting yesterday behind you and never retracing your steps. You are stimulated by worldly experience and anxious to take part in the competition. Daring and unafraid, you plunge forward into tomorrow. Note in the sample below how the *i* dot is placed far ahead of the stroke and that the *t* crossing bar is longer on the right side than the left. The increased width of the left-hand margin shows an impatience to get further forward.

This new company will earn a profit of 2 millions the first year and 6 millions the second!

Forward Direction   Yes ___ No ___

If you write in a neutral direction you are always sizing up a situation before acting on it, making moves which are calculated and prices. You weigh the pros and cons, and may then make no move at all in preference to making a wrong one. Careful and cautious, your projected goals are often delayed or never materialize at all. You are not easily persuaded to act on the notions of other people. When you attempt anything, you accept sole responsibility for it. Self-assertive, your primary aim is to satisfy the standards you set for yourself and which you have found to be safe.

The handwriting sample shows an upright slant, with the *t* bar crossed evenly on both sides of the stem and the *i* dotted directly over the stroke. The margins are even and well organized:

When the children are grown, we will move to Florida and look for a small business there.

Neutral Direction   Yes ___ No ___

The backward direction is a sign that any movement toward goals recognized and accepted in the structured society are retarded. You reject and ignore standardized goals and also the people who live by them, and are intolerant of systems and organized patterns. You move toward highly personalized objectives, resenting those imposed upon you by other people. Actually, you are afraid of the future and seek refuge in your own past thoughts and acts. The sample shows the movements leaning backward in the slant, the *t* crossing, the *i* dot, and the withdrawing margin.

I can't justif the establishment. the pollution problem and over population — or what is there to look forward to?

Backward Direction   Yes ___ No ___

If you score high in speed and force and indicate a forward direction, you are a person with abounding energy, active in both thought and motion. Nothing can stop you or get in your way. You overcome obstacles quickly and forcefully, approaching goals with great enthusiasm and staying power to see them through. Other people admire and look to you for guidance and leadership, respecting your authority and having confidence in your ability to see that projects are carried out to a successful conclusion.

You are always projecting into the future. Before one project is accomplished, you are anticipating and acting on the next one. You are impulsive and attempt challenging situations, especially those involving people. People are attracted to you, but also wary, as they find you a little threatening and overwhelming. You don't have time to indulge in self-pity or regret for things you have already done, for you are too busy moving on. No one person can keep up with you and you do not wait for them to meet your pace, so you divert your energies into different areas where many people can participate with you in varied situations.

The greatest difficulty you encounter is learning how to rest or even to relax in nonserious pastimes, for you are conditioned to a state that is always in high gear. Your leisure time is spent in pleasures of a competitive nature and in many ways resembles the things you do to earn a living. You are not a spectator in life or in play, but a doer and achiever.

The above description will give you a gauge for measuring your own action-mindedness and how it is demonstrated in your everyday actions. The possible combinations are too many to cite individually here, but you can easily arrive at an evaluation of yourself by combining the characteristics of your writing.

List here your score, as it will be valuable later when you look at your total personality.

Speed _____

Force _____

Direction _____

Now go back to the questionnaire on pages 53-54 and compare what you discovered in your handwriting with what you felt was true about you. This should give you fuel for thought, and hopefully help you work toward a freer and more comfortable physical self.

4.

you, the thinker

This is neither a challenge nor a judgment, but only an exercise to make you sit back and consider the sort of thinker you believe you are. You may overestimate or under-credit your thinking abilities in this questionnaire. In becoming more aware both of your weaknesses and strengths, you can remove a lot of your frustrations and project goals that are realistic and have a greater chance for success.

Yes	No	?	
——	——	——	1. Are you perceptive and able to solve problems quickly?
——	——	——	2. Are you a plodder and do you accumulate information until you have enough facts to make a decision?
——	——	——	3. Do you have good powers of concentration?
——	——	——	4. Does intuition greatly influence your thinking?
——	——	——	5. Do you rely upon the opinion of others?
——	——	——	6. Do you have a naturally good memory?

Yes   No   ?

   7. Are you able to think a few moves ahead?

   8. Do you look for new approaches in developing ideas?

   9. Do you try to handle too many things at one time?

   10. Does your mind work so rapidly that other people have trouble trying to keep up with you?

   11. Is your thinking slower than average so you have problems in keeping up with others?

   12. Do you consider yourself intelligent?

   13. Is your normal thinking disturbed when you are upset?

   14. Is your mind working at its level of capability?

No one fully understands the complicated process of thinking, and it would be presumptuous to make absolute statements about how thinking develops. There has been a great deal of research and certain theories have become widely accepted. A child's thinking advances in stages. He learns to think and perform in accordance with his body and mind maturation level. Studies have shown that attempts to teach advanced skills such as reading, writing, music, and dance most frequently did not result in the acceleration of the child over a period of a few years. The child who was taught a particular skill at the normal stage of preparedness was just as adept as the one who had received earlier training.

The old cliché that you must learn to crawl before you walk has of late been given serious consideration. There are some schools in psychotherapy which actually teach children and adults to crawl because they had never crawled in infancy. The theory is that, if they missed this step in early development, it may have caused their psychomotor problem and that filling in the gap might cure it.

In respect to the factors of heredity, growth, and environment, a way of thinking may become a habit. Through years of reinforcing, the memory cells become very difficult to change—though not impossible. Your thinking interacts with your physical and emotional forces, and all together they form habit patterns which reflect your personality. As long as you have a body, you can never be a totally free thinker. The mind is too influenced by the physical desires of the body ever to act freely. For a thought pattern to change, the corresponding gesture and emotion must change with it. A patient undergoing analysis and therapy is encouraged not only to understand his problems, but also to begin to accept them emotionally and then create actual physical conditions conducive to desirable change. It took a long time to develop unfavorable thinking habits, therefore, time is necessary to change them to favorable habits. Unusual circumstances or emotional shock can bring about a startling change in attitude. The loss of health or a loved one can change a happy outgoing personality to a bitter and withdrawn one. Successful experiences giving confidence and ego strength frequently change attitudes from negative to positive. The most reliable method for desirable change of thinking habits is first to face honestly your present characteristics, recognize the weaknesses and the strengths, then provide favorable conditions where change can be acted upon.

Your general pattern of thinking is discernible in your handwriting. It is observable in the letter shapes (the motivation symbols), writing speed (action mindedness), and the size of the three writing zones.

The triangular-shaped letters are the key to whether or not you are this type thinker. Your pen arrives at a point which your mind has already grasped. This point probes and explores with sharp agility, gathering quick impressions from which rapid decisions are made. You approach ideas and problems with directness and keen perception. Note the quick movement of this sample and the sharp triangular points in the *m, n, t, d,* and *s.*

This method is basically sound .

Small middle-zone letters, less than one-eighth inch in height, which are clear and legibly written, indicate good concentrative ability. You are able to hold on to one thought without being invaded by other images and ideas. Your attention span is good and you work with mental precision and organization. You are self-disciplined in controlling and directing your mental energies.

You prefer to work out your thoughts in solitude and do not

require assurances and stimulation from others to apply yourself to the task.

I have been working on this one idea.

When your pen races quickly across the page, it is because your mind is working so rapidly that the hand attempts to keep up the pace. It is unusual to encounter handwritings which are both rapid and clearly legible. There is generally some sacrifice made of the less important quality. However rare, it does exist. If you are one of the remarkable few who think with tremendous speed and clarity, you are mentally productive and communicative.

haven't had time to check

A practical mind assesses information and arrives at a solution based upon what the facts indicate is the right answer. If you have a reasoning mind, you do not rely upon insight or intuition. You weigh all possibilities before making judgment. Whether this pattern of thinking is fast or slow, sound or fallible, it is still your way. You take the time to sort and evaluate your thoughts. No matter how adept or well trained you are at assessing them, your thinking is not spontaneous. You are aware of contributing factors to situations and consider them in your ultimate conclusions.

When appraising anything you are aware of its total form, but your mind moves around the periphery to investigate its separate parts. This is the same approach you use in outlining letter forms. You don't take shortcuts nor do you inflate your movements. Your forms are conservatively between round and square. Note the broad tops of the *n, m, r,* and *v*. The *t* is crossed with an umbrella-like stroke showing flexibility for reasoning. Unfortunately, it also suggests a mind that can be swayed from its purpose. The reasoning person carries the burden of having to consider more than the impulsive or rigid thinker.

Why do you want to marry me?

Small and well-defined middle-zone letters add weight to your power of logic by its indication that you are able to concentrate, keeping a mental hold on the subject at thought. You are not side-tracked by irrelevancy but use only meaningful information in figuring out a situation.

This man is a poor credit risk.

If you are a logical thinker, quick in your reasoning, and able to concentrate, you have the qualities of being a judge, lawyer, philosopher, educator, administrator, or any other role requiring quick and valued judgment.

Early rigid training and discipline can often be a detriment to mental growth and independent thinking. Conversely, it can act as a solid foundation and reservoir of strength to draw from in developing patterns of thinking. The danger lies in becoming dependent upon the direction of other people because not enough freedom has been allowed the child to learn to make his own decisions. This does not strengthen confidence and self-image, but develops a habit of looking to others as a more reliable authority. If you lack confidence in your own ideas, you will not be stimulated to produce them and much of your inherent abilities to create will be stifled in the bud.

When you first learned to write in school, you obediently attempted to trace the outline of letters from the blackboard as the teacher instructed. As your manipulative skill improved, you were able to reproduce the letters with more exactness. If authority was strict at home and at school, and you responded to it without defiance throughout your growing years, this condition is not likely to change in adulthood. Your handwriting will continue to conform to the principles and exact patterns learned as a child.

Your continued adherence to early training and moral discipline is seen when you still use beginning and ending strokes to letters, and the size relationship of the upper, middle, and lower zones will not have changed appreciably. Your capitals, as well as other letters, will have the appearance of the school model. This is not necessarily a stamp of immaturity, but can be a rigid attitude regarding ethics, morality, and social responsibility to family and community. Immaturity is apparent when these writing characteristics are combined with oversized middle-zone letters which are very circular.

DEPENDENT MATURE THINKER

I'm happy my work satisfies you.

DEPENDENT IMMATURE THINKER

Show me how you want it done.

The dependent mature thinker can be a valuable employee, for he follows instructions and does not rebel against routine and repetitious details. If your writing fits the above description, you will not resent being subordinate and will cooperate with superiors to gain their approval. This is your potential. Whether or not you meet it depends upon other factors. Speed is an element which can work for or against you. In performing routine tasks, it is a real asset. However, you will tend to impose upon your own children the same strict discipline that you received without consideration for the changing environment outside the home. You find it difficult to participate in these changes yourself. Whatever your age, you are on the senior side of the generation gap.

Intelligence can be defined simply as the potential for learning and the ability to put into use what is learned. All living organisms have a degree of intelligence or they would not be able to survive. A true evaluation of intelligence through modern testing procedures is difficult to ascertain, even with the Environment Free examinations. This is because the emotional and physical condition of the person being tested may greatly influence his performance. Overanxiousness, fear, a premonition of failure, and generally not feeling well will have a bearing on the final score and it will not reflect an accurate picture of the true abilities.

Your handwriting is also affected by your feeling physically or emotionally upset, and it is a warning for you to sit up and take note when you see this in your writing, for you may not be otherwise aware that something is bothering you. The graphologist determines if this is a normal or temporary condition by comparing two samples written at different times. Here are significant indications of intelligence in handwriting.

An astute mind will take a complicated situation and strip it down to its basic essentials. When you remove all the trimmings of a problem, you can more clearly see the core of it and begin to solve it from there. You will note how these letter forms are reduced to a basic structure and still maintain their essential character.

I've solved the problem, you do the rest!

A good memory is extremely valuable. Some memory is vital to intelligence, for how would you measure anyone's mental ability if he had no memory of the things he learned? A good memory furnishes the mind's consciousness with information and eliminates the time-consuming need to search it out again. It is a conveniently useful tool in saving time and effort. The wide speculation is that good memory patterns develop through interest, attention, concentration, and repetition. Poor retention can be improved by developing the habit of thought association, word and number keys, and just by mentally alerting yourself to remember. Much has been expounded on by experts like Bruno Furst, James D. Weinland, and Harry Lorraine, who have certainly contributed much to memory improvement methods.

Albert Einstein was notably absentminded, yet no one questions that he possessed a brilliant mind. What he considered trivia, he discarded from his memory, allowing room for greater thought.

Remembering to cross your *t*'s, dot your *i*'s and *j*'s, and put in the proper punctuation marks—as well as remembering how to spell commonly used words—is evidence of a naturally good memory. You have the ability to make use of it in broad areas, providing you remove any inhibiting hang-ups.

GOOD MEMORY

You said on Dec. 5, 1962, "I will buy you a grey mink stole."

POOR MEMORY

It was a great memory couse but but I forgot who gave it.

Anticipation is the ability to project your thinking further ahead from what is happening at the moment. While driving a car you may approach a child on a bicycle. You anticipate the possibility that the child might veer the bicycle in front of your car, so you almost automatically slow down and move broadly around the child. You roll up the windows of your car when clouds appear and the sky darkens and perhaps carry an umbrella, you shop for more food when expecting a house guest, take out life and health insurance, and prejudge the time you will need for the day's activities. The anticipator is never far behind, late for an appointment, or in a frenzy to keep up with his schedule. He gauges how much time it will take him to arrive at a destination or to complete a task, always allowing time for unexpected interruptions. He is less accident-prone, prepared for the second step while still taking the first. He experiences fewer surprises and shocks, and has a sure footing for sound judgment.

When you anticipate the second stroke of a letter while still writing the first, both will be consistent in size, and spaces between the letters equaled. You are prejudging the character and value of letters and giving them proper relationship to one another. Relating letter size, shape, and space is analogous to relating pieces of information until a complete idea is formed. In your handwriting, you move from one letter to the next until a word is formed and then a complete thought which is to be communicated to someone.

ANTICIPATION

No sense cleaning before the party, it's sure to get dirty.

LACK OF ANTICIPATION

"What, he's your husband and not your son?"

The intangible quality intuition is frequently misunderstood, for it is believed to be an inborn talent. You get an immediate feeling of like or dislike about someone, or you intuitively feel that you should or should not do a particular thing, that something will or will not be successful, and you attribute all these feelings to intuition. Actually, the mind is like an IBM computer, gathering impressions, ideas, and information. A question is fed into it, and the memory banks so rapidly calculate an answer and supply it to you that you attribute this phenomenon to intuition. Some people wake up every morning at a planned time without the aid of an alarm clock because their level of unconsciousness is ticking away the minutes and hours. You may intuitively make the right decisions, but if you search deep enough you will find the real reasons which led you to them.

Though there may be a mysterious guiding hand, intuition is most often the quick, unconscious processing of stored-up information which alerts you to answers before you have an opportunity to think them out consciously. If your mind operates with this definition of intuition, many of your letters will be disconnected. You complete a letter form and lift your pen to begin the next letter at exactly the right place and distance from the preceding one. Your mind quickly and accurately calculates and your hand responds, for the unconscious mechanism is efficient and working for you.

I have a feeling she doesn't trust me!

Our early school experiences teach us to make separate groups of thoughts so they don't confuse and overwhelm us. We are shown how to plan our work beginning with simple procedures involving limited tasks. As we mature, we gain greater independence and begin to develop our own study and work patterns.

An adaptable child responds well to this training, carrying to adulthood the facility of clear and well-organized thinking. The ability to communicate ideas increases, and time is saved allowing for greater productivity. It is not true that organized people are dull and unexciting. Some of the greatest minds and talents give evidence that planning and organization are essential to creating great works. Beethoven's nine symphonies are masterfully structured, Michelangelo's paintings on the ceilings of the Sistine Chapel were planned and scaled, and Plato's Dialogues reflect highly organized thought.

If your handwriting is well organized on the sheet of paper, it will be immediately observed by the reader. The left-hand margin will be even all the way down, except for paragraph indentations, and the right-hand margin will have very little variation. Spaces will be ample and precise, separating one word from another so that each stands out clearly.

ORGANIZED THINKING

Sweet heart,
Your dinner is in the oven. Turn it on to 450°.
for 20 minutes. I will be home at 8:30. The
movie begins at 9, and we can see the show.

DISORGANIZED THINKING

Dear Jane,
I might be home for dinner, but I'm
not sure. If I can get away I'll call you,
if not, wait for me anyway.

Your Thinking Evaluation

Check the characteristics you have seen in your handwriting. If conflicting traits appear, choose the ones which are the most frequent in your writing sample.

____ Probing and penetrating
____ Concentrative ability
____ Agility
____ Reasoning and logical
____ Dependent (mature)
____ Dependent (immature)
____ Problem solving

____ Memory (good)
____ Memory (poor)
____ Anticipation (good)
____ Anticipation (poor)
____ Intuition
____ Organization (good)
____ Organization (poor)

This will give you a good view of your thinking patterns as revealed in your handwriting. Then go back to the questionnaire on pages 66-67 and compare.

5.

you, the social animal

The following characteristics are considered social traits because they depend upon interplay and involvement with other people. If you believe a particular trait is dominant in your personality, and not a minor one, you are to check the "Yes" column.

Yes	No	?		Yes	No	?	
—	—	—	Extrovert	—	—	—	Optimistic
—	—	—	Introvert	—	—	—	Pessimistic
—	—	—	Moral	—	—	—	Shy
—	—	—	Amoral	—	—	—	Ostentatious
—	—	—	Generous	—	—	—	Procrastinator
—	—	—	Conservative	—	—	—	Ambitious
—	—	—	Frugal	—	—	—	Lazy
—	—	—	Humorous	—	—	—	Proud
—	—	—	Witty	—	—	—	Vain
—	—	—	Sarcastic	—	—	—	Humble
—	—	—	Stubborn	—	—	—	Self-Confident
—	—	—	Yielding	—	—	—	Impatient

Yes	No	?				
___	___	___	Resentful	___	___	___ Cautious
___	___	___	Compassionate	___	___	___ Deceitful
___	___	___	Inconsiderate	___	___	___ Honest

An interesting social game is to have friends complete this sheet on someone else at a party. It will be a very short party!

The social animal is the you that everyone sees, the personality which shows a visible image to the public. Few people, probably yourself included, take the time to probe into the underlying reasons for social behavior. They are content in accepting what they see on the surface when they judge themselves and others, labeling the personality with one-word descriptions. People are referred to as extrovert or introvert, ambitious or lazy, good-natured or bad-humored, intelligent or dull, generous or greedy, and so on down the line.

The outward impressions of a personality may be misleading or entirely untrue. Our behavior toward individuals is largely guided by what we think of them, and if we judge by superficial factors alone, we may be doing them and ourselves an injustice. You would not judge a man guilty of an act before knowing the circumstances involved, nor would you praise a man's philanthropy if you learned he earned his wealth through drug traffic operations.

When I worked for public welfare in Philadelphia, I frequently visited an aged woman who was receiving financial assistance. She lived alone in a one-room, sparsely furnished apartment and was suffering with tuberculosis of the bone. Pathetically lonely and desperate, she spoke to me frequently of her three children who hadn't visited her for years nor given her any financial help or comfort. I decided to make a search for the daughter and two sons. At the office I pulled out the reserve file on her case, which contained earlier information. After reading it, the impression I had of the poor and lonely sick woman who was abandoned by her children completely changed. The three children were born out of wedlock, fathered by three different men. Soon after giving birth, she abandoned them and they were shifted around in various foster homes until old enough to leave and earn a living for themselves. The woman, wanted by the police for a number of offenses, moved from place to place to avoid being apprehended. Thinking of her in her present condition, with a Bible by her side, it was difficult to imagine the ruthless selfishness of this woman's life. I had condemned the children before looking further into the situation.

Undoubtedly you can recall times when you have changed your mind about a person after you got to know him better, or someone changed his mind about you.

The dictionary defines an extrovert as one who turns his mind outward and is interested in the physical and social environment. The true extrovert is involved mentally and emotionally with people, community, government, and the role he plays within this society. He is aware of what is happening in the world and wants to take part in it. Concerned with relating to the action around him, he wants to play, work, and communicate with people.

The extrovert is gregarious and wants to be with people both at work and during his periods of leisure, is comfortable in their company, and has developed an easy rapport with them. People not only give him pleasure, but they also make him feel secure and feed his ego—this is why they are so much a part of almost everything he does. If you are an extrovert, it often appears that you give more to another than you take from him, but you are more than compensated by the affection and acceptance you receive. You follow timely and popular issues and get pleasure from exchanging your views with others. You are sensitive and hurt whenever excluded by friends, family, and associates. As you have developed your interests to include people, you are bored and unhappy when alone.

The handwriting indications of gregariousness are slant, shape, and pressure. The slant reveals the emotional outward movement toward others (forward), the shape shows the love you have for them (circle), and the pressure indicates the intensity of your feelings (heavy pressure).

GREGARIOUSNESS

Invite them all, we'll make room.

The extrovert calls attention to himself because he wants recognition. If you are an extrovert, you are intent upon making your presence known to others. You may speak out your opinions, head committees, champion causes, be the life of the party, and respond to situations which draw the eyes and ears of people to focus upon you.

The handwriting is large and dark, so that it can be easily seen. The pressure need not necessarily be great, but you will use a writing tool that produces a thick dark stroke.

RECOGNITION

Well, if you really want me to, I accept!

You need self-confidence, though you may not have it, to distinguish yourself from the crowd. Since you often volunteer yourself to the limelight you are subject to the challenge of maintaining your image once committed to a position. You may be aware of certain vulnerabilities and inadequacies, but rather than back out you will assure yourself that you can handle the project you have taken on. You emphasize the importance of what you do and your ability—— making you the best one to do it.

Exclamation marks and underscoring of words are sure signs of fostering self-confidence. Further, underscoring your own signature is a dead giveaway.

SELF-CONFIDENCE

"I go on record as saying—!"

James Wright

The introvert is involved with his own thoughts and feelings, as they are turned inward to himself. He does not relate easily to other people, since he doesn't identify his own thoughts and feelings with theirs. Getting through to him is difficult, for he hasn't the knack for developing lines of communication to send or receive signals which are generally understood.

If you are an introvert, you are restrained and uncomfortable with groups of two or more. You avoid social gatherings, but if thrown into one you will find a quiet corner and be less distressed. You may seek a haven in avant-garde groups where you can hide and not play the social game, but it acts more as a shelter from others than a desire to be with certain type people. As an introvert, you have more opportunity to be creative and productive than the extrovert, for you are less concerned with social pressures and keeping up with the standard of living.

The characteristics of the introvert result from developed attitudes toward people. There are some salient traits which are found in the handwriting.

Though you are actually withdrawing from others, you often feel that they are rejecting you. You lean backward and away from them, suspicious and mistrusting. You wonder what they want from you, and what you might be compelled to give. You may appear to be shy and timid, but these are traits of modesty not of withdrawal, and not truly characteristic of the introvert. The shy person is often very humble and lacking in self-confidence, but wants very much to be able to enjoy the company of other people.

The reasons for not developing the normal extrovertish characteristics are many and varied. An inadequate early homelife with weak parent image or fear of parents can readily cause the child to transfer these feelings to the world at large. If in childhood you were bitter and resentful and felt threatened in both the home and school environment, it would not be easy to develop responsive and outgoing feelings toward others in adulthood. Feeling undesirable and unworthy may cause you to build a wall of defense around yourself, shutting yourself in and everyone else out.

The writing slant is backward in emotional withdrawal from people. Strong pressure indicates an adamant determination to reject those who try to approach too closely.

WITHDRAWAL

I like people who leave me alone.

If you are uncommunicative you do not demonstrate your feelings or reveal your thoughts freely. When you do, it is with hesitation and constraint, for you are suspicious that what you reveal might be used as ammunition in an attack against you. Your letters in writing are closed tightly, leaving no gaps and vulnerable openings. The circle letters *a, o,* and *d* may show reinforcing loops to make sure that nobody can get through.

UNCOMMUNICATIVE

I have nothing more to add to what I've said.

Your attitude on morals and ethics will also show in your handwriting. Some people profess to live by their own code of principles and moral values, not those set by the society. But most of us regard laws as made by the group to protect individual rights and conform in order that our own freedoms are not violated. Some people are rigid about adhering strictly to the letter of the law and to learned principles of right and wrong. Others show flexibility within the structured codes of the society and allow themselves greater latitude to interpret what is right and wrong.

For the strict moralist something is either right or wrong. There are no shades of gray. You follow the straight and narrow road along the journey of life, demanding of yourself, as well as others, prudent behavior. You are always concerned about doing and saying the right thing, and will avoid situations which might tend to provoke unpleasant gossip about you. You are neat, orderly, and exacting, becoming distressed when things are not in the proper place or a responsibility not carried out when it should have been.

You are reliable and can be depended upon without reminders or extra incentives, accepting obligations as a duty in life. The more frivolous will not find you very broad-minded, but serious and critical. You do tend to overemphasize the trivial, giving it greater importance than it deserves. Steadfast and loyal to people and causes you believe are good and right, you will be less forgiving to them when you see their weaknesses.

If you reflect a strictly moral individual, your handwriting will show exacting attention to every detail. Note in the sample how close to the stem the *i*'s are dotted and the equal length of the *t* bar crossing on both sides of the stem. The period at the end of the sentence appears precisely where the last word stroke ends. There is little variation in letter forms from the early writing instruction in school, as basic principles have not changed:

STRICT MORALITY

I sent out invitations and then notified everyone by phone.

If you are a liberal moralist, you question the existing social standards and then interpret them in such a way that they are compatible with your own principles. Aware of responsibilities and obligations to self, family, and community, you allow yourself a broader scope for ways to carry them out. You are not a gossiper nor petty about small things, and feel that people should be able to do their own thing without censure and criticism as long as they do not hurt others. You prefer to judge the end result of a project rather than look at the small individual parts. You feel the same way about people, accepting them for what they are and unconcerned about their small idiosyncrasies. Wishing that others would react similarly to you and your work, you are still not devastated by their disapproval. Your motto is not to be tied down by insignificancies when there are important things in life to be concerned about.

In your handwriting you pay attention to important details but are more liberal about what you do with them. The *i* and *j* dots will be freely placed but near enough to define the meaning of the letter, as well as commas and other punctuation marks. Printed and written letters will appear together, as you are not confined strictly to the letter of the law in handwriting either. You do not erase or retrace a letter which is not written legibly when you feel that the word will be understood anyway. Movement is free and spacious.

LIBERAL MORALITY

His political views don't disturb the good work he does.

Those who disregard the ethical codes which govern the society will, by action or inaction, be destructive to the welfare of the community. Crimes are committed by people who defy laws, but there are other kinds of amorality. They may be more subtle and less sensational, but nonetheless they demonstrate the lack of morality. During the Second World War certain American businesses sold defective strategic materials to the armed forces which resulted in the added loss of many lives. Others traded with the enemy for profit. Unions have negotiated privately with big business, leaving both the workers and consumers the victims. Many a man has deserted his wife and children, leaving them with no means of support. Physicians will carelessly diagnose and prescribe while knowing they could and should examine the patient further.

In the first years of learning to write you are taught basic principles. As you continue to develop, you learn the rules for structuring complete and more complicated thoughts. The degree to which you defy or ignore these rules indicates your attitude toward discipline and authority. In the sample you will notice the absence of punctuation marks and the deliberate distortion of letter forms. The unusual placed gaps in the *a*'s and *o*'s further indicate an unwillingness to give what is expected.

AMORALITY

I promise to change Please take me back.

When you gain pleasure from giving of yourself and your possessions, you are generous. The gesture is spontaneous and unplanned. It springs from the desire to extend a hand to another human being. Sharing things which belong to you increases their value, for you then also enjoy the pleasure they give to others. When you write to someone you are offering your words and thoughts. Your generosity is shown by how willing and liberal you are in giving them.

You use space freely between letters, words, lines, and margins. The strokes ending words will swing round and upward as if you were stretching your hand out to the reader.

GENEROSITY

Don't worry, just pay me when you can.

The economy-minded individual will conserve space and movement wherever possible. Narrow margins, cramped letters, and lines close together show that the writer is conserving space and paper. The writing will begin at the top of the page and continue very close to the bottom before a new sheet is begun. Often two sides of the paper will be used in order to save weight and an additional postage stamp. The writer wants to get as much as possible from the materials used, so he sacrifices his freedom of movement in order to economize. Small writing does not necessarily indicate a motive to conserve space. It may be very free and generous but styled to fit other characteristics of the writer. Large writing can be cramped and inhibited as this example shows:

FRUGALITY

I am returning the stockings. After wearing them only three times, one stocking ripped. Please send full refund at once of $1.95, plus $.06 tax.

People who like to laugh also enjoy making other people laugh. If you have a sense of humor you have the ability to find something funny in a serious situation and make it less unhappy. Your jokes and repartee have the quality of bringing smiles to faces, not frowns, and people enjoy your company. When pressures mount and problems become oppressive, you have your sense of humor to fall back on.

The circle, symbolizing love, play, and pleasure is found in the accouterments of the letter forms, not necessarily the letters themselves, for a sense of humor is an accessory of the personality and not one of the basic parts. The circle is used frivolously in circling the *i* and *j* dots, the beginning of capitals, and in the swing of upper loops. It says, "Let's have some fun while we live."

SENSE OF HUMOR

Of course the knives are heated, it saves butter.

Take a sense of humor, stir intelligence into it, and you will find a person with a wit. If you can show the true nature of a happening with a funny twist to it, you have what is called sophisticated humor or wit. It is a valuable and delightful characteristic, one which stimulates and impresses many people. Good comedians train themselves to capture the truths in people and situations, and then cleverly apply their humor to it.

In addition to the humor circles, the handwriting will show the intelligence of simplified letter forms.

WIT

Man is descendant of the apes, and has been descending ever since.

This characteristic does not cause people to laugh, especially when it is directed toward them. Sarcasm is geared at finding and expressing fault in a devious and unflattering way. The perpetrator perhaps finds it funny, but his words are pointed arrows intended to sting when hitting their targets. Observe the arrow-pointed *t* bar crossing, *i* dots, and punctuation marks.

SARCASM

You're stunning for your age!

If you hold firmly to what you think and feel even in the light of reason and rationality, you are surely stubborn. Once your mind is made up nothing can change it, for your thoughts are tied so tightly that they cannot be unraveled. When you make a decision, you commit yourself to stand by it, and are unhappy if you are forced to retract it.

The *t* strokes and lower loops are tied in a knot. Dots and punctuation are strong and assertive. Word-ending strokes are cut off with strong finality. Yet, Shakespeare says "for who so firm that cannot be seduced . . . ?"

STUBBORNNESS

I'm not going to call him first.

You are yielding and able to give in because you've never completely closed your mind to anything. Your convictions are not so firm that they cannot move their position. Flexibility and openness allow you to yield to reason without damaging your values and ego.

The handwriting will show resiliency in the *s* and *p* as they are not closed up tightly at the base line. There is no concerted effort to close up the small rounded letter forms *a, o,* and *d.* The writer is unsuspicious and does not feel threatened, leaving himself vulnerable and wide open for attack.

YIELDING

We don't have children, but the diapers were on sale.

When you feel imposed upon, you may either react immediately and show your resentment, or you may store it up within and carry it along with you for a time. You harbor ill feelings toward those you feel are in some way abusing you and seek some form of retaliation, even if it is only a mentally compensating one. You question the motives of others when they ask something of you, and you usually look for something in return.

Many of the upmoving strokes begin from below the base line and are heavy and rigid. Ending word strokes close down under the base line with the same strength of rigidity.

RESENTFUL

Tell me now what you want to see me about.

The compassionate person is sensitive to the feelings of others. He feels their embarrassments and hurts and will try to comfort them. If you are compassionate with other human beings, you understand and sympathize with their plights and sorrows and identify with their deeper emotions. You have a delicate tuning-in device which picks up the subtle feelings of other people. When they turn to you, you will help them.

The writing pressure is light, indicating sensitivity. The middle zone of writing will be relatively larger than the upper and lower ones, for it represents the body of society, which is most important to you. The slant direction is forward and the general movement of letter forms is circular. You will find this consistent with the love motivation symbol.

COMPASSIONATE

I visited your mother in the hospital, and she's feeling much better.

When you receive a letter which is scribbled and difficult to read, you know that the sender is lacking in consideration. He is unconcerned about your time and effort in attempting to read it. A line of writing which looks like a radio wave is a sign that the writer wants to get his message through quickly regardless of whether or not it is understood. You don't have to be a graphologist to detect the more obvious signs which show lack of consideration. Sending a letter on memo sheets or scratch paper, the use of a pencil in place of a pen, no return address or zip code on the envelope, and insufficient postage are indications of lack of thought for others. Being remiss about just one of these details is not evidence of this characteristic, but when two or more signs appear there is little question that inconsideration exists. Note how you must strain to understand these samples:

INCONSIDERATE

Please understand why I can't the invitations appears to be a member

Always looking upward and on the brighter side, the optimist is sure that everything will turn out right. If you are an optimist you find some value even in an unhappy or unsuccessful venture. Nothing defeats you. You try again, or move upward to something new and just as rewarding.

Your enthusiasm generates physical energy which you use to move your hand continuously uphill as you write. This movement is unconscious, as it is really your intention to follow a straight course across the page. However, your high-spirited nature and positive thinking carry you progressively above the invisible base line.

OPTIMISTIC

I know we'll love California and make many new friends. The new job is exciting

To qualify as a pessimist you must have the attitude that there is more chance for failure than for success. This apprehension depresses and defeats you before even beginning a venture. Your premonition of not succeeding robs you of energy and enthusiasm. This in turn weakens your spirit and causes your performance to lag behind your capability.

Your hand loses energy as it moves across the page, pulling the writing down and giving the impression of a sinking ship. Downhill writing sometimes reflects a temporary unhappy mood, and when the mood changes back to a normal condition, the handwriting will climb upward again. Physical illness and fatigue also cause downhill writing. After suffering a heart attack, a man can hardly lift a pen, much less move it evenly or uphill across a sheet of paper. It is easy to determine if illness is the cause of downhill writing, as there is corroborating evidence such as alternating pressure, unsteady letter formations, breaks and jutting-out points in the strokes, and general lack of control of the writing.

This sample shows pessimism where no illness is causing it:

PESSIMISTIC

Everything I seem to do goes wrong. I guess I just have bad luck!

If you are shy, you are not necessarily an introvert. Your timidity stems from the embarrassment you feel in situations with people, and being uncomfortable you hide a little. You are uncertain about yourself and how people react to you. When encouraged and reassured, you come out of the shell and respond willingly and warmly.

You underestimate yourself and play down your attributes with genuine modesty, while you overestimate the qualities of others. This places you in your own mind as being less adequate and capable than they. Fear of rejection inhibits you from taking the lead in developing a relationship; you wait for others to make the first move. You do not challenge nor compete, though you might be more capable of winning than those who do. On the surface, people view you as likable and unthreatening. They are surprised when they see your strengths in non-people situations.

Shyness is indicated by small and unpretentious writing. Capitals are the strongest evidence of this characteristic. They bear no embellishments and are much reduced from the standard size.

SHYNESS

My sister is beautiful and talented. She can do almost anything. I was always clumsy.

You are ostentatious because you seek the admiration and envy from others. You may do any number of things to accomplish this, depending upon the kind of attention you are looking for. Showing off material possessions, flamboyancy of dress, publicized contributions, name dropping, and generally going out of the way to make people aware of you are characteristic of this trait.

The handwriting is large, so that nobody can miss seeing it. Capitals and letters ending the sentence will have superfluous additions, which have nothing to do with the meaning of the letter. They are there to draw more attention.

OSTENTATION

My voice is a little scratchy, but I'll be happy to sing.

Your ambition is seen by others in the strength of your will and determination to succeed in everything you undertake. You don't idly wait for opportunities to come your way, you go out and make them, but you are also alert and recognize an opportunity when it happens along. Ambition is a self-motivating force; nobody talks it into you. You push ahead through obstacles and adversity because you are driven by an inner energy.

There are three writing indices which together total the characteristic of ambition.

AMBITION

STRONG WILL: The *t* stroke crossing is firm and unbending and also shows heavy pressure. Word-ending letters are blunt and unyielding. Dots are emphatic and unreversible.

I stopped smoking ten years ago.

DETERMINATION: The *t* stroke is long, following through past the ensuing letters. Lower loops are long and straight, indicating staying power and patience to keep going.

Put them on overtime, but get the job done!

DRIVE: Writing pressure is strong, carrying weight of purpose. The end of a stroke will be even heavier than beginning and middle movements, indicating that you have a reserve of energy available and that your finish is as strong or stronger than your beginnings.

In ten years, I'll own the company!

WILL, DETERMINATION, AND DRIVE: These three are the determinants of ambition. They are interrelated and only valuable when they work together as a unit. Here is the sample writing of a truly ambitious person:

*The time is now to buy out
Support !*

The major cause of laziness is indifference and lack of stimulation. In this context, a person is considered lazy when unmotivated in everything he does. Movements are slow and uninspired, and whatever energy is generated is small and renewed at a very slow rate. If you are lazy, you fatigue easily and feel overburdened with activity which would be considered normal for others. You might actually be operating at your true level of activeness, but it is more likely that an emotional barrier is preventing a higher degree of performance. It is well to consider both possibilities. A physical examination can determine the health factor, and frequently the handwriting reveals the existence of such a problem.

The writing speed is slow and lacks any strength of pressure. The *t* strokes are short, placed low across the bar, and curved. Punctuation marks are particularly light and carelessly placed. Writing corrections are made by retracing the correct letter or word over the wrong one, rather than taking time to erase or begin again.

LAZINESS

*I must get up early tomorrow and collect
my unemployment check*

Pride is the trait of those who hold themselves above the common mass. They protect themselves with a shield of invulnerability because they have a fear that their human weaknesses might be revealed to others. If you are proud, you are not at ease in accepting help and comfort, for it injures your personal integrity and estimated self-worth.

The pride referred to here is a general characteristic of a person and not the pleasant, healthy feelings of pride of achievement, pride in loved ones, and pride in what you are as an individual. The proud person is overly concerned about public commentary and wants to be regarded with high esteem. He pays bills promptly, incurs no obligations, invites after having been invited, does not admit to personal failure, and shows his background and heritage as one beyond disrepute.

The handwriting indicates high-mindedness by the *d* and *t* stems rising high above the middle-zone letters. The middle zone represents the "social" body.

PRIDE

We drive a Cadillac, not a Dodge.

When the high *d* and *t* stems are also inflated, the writer is inflating his pride which swells up into vanity. He wants everyone to see what he himself is proud of, so he not only raises these letters high but blows them up bigger than all the rest.

VANITY

They made me play 3 encores, untill I got it right.

If you have humility you are aware that whatever you have and whatever you have achieved has to some measure been made possible by many people. Men who have distinguished themselves by their great minds and talents, and whose contributions are enjoyed by the whole society, feel and show humility. They know and appreciate the opportunities given them by the common people. Humility is a characteristic of mature understanding that one man depends upon another no matter how great is his talent and ability.

In the handwriting, the *d* and *t* strokes do not rise far above the common middle-zone letters. They feel a closer relationship and meet almost on the same level. The stems are short and uninflated.

HUMILITY

I deeply appreciate your asking my advice on the matter.

True self-confidence comes from experiencing more successes than failures and so developing the habit of feeling you will be successful in your undertakings. It is the memory of past failures which destroys confidence and creates a fear to attempt again. If you have real self-confidence, you do not see yourself as a failure when not achieving a particular goal. Only your part in that particular action has failed, not you as a person.

If you are self-assured, unthreatened by doubts of your adequacy, you have the advantage of being able to analyze a failure, see what went wrong, and use this knowledge to help in the future. You are sufficiently objective to evaluate both your weaknesses and strengths, and thus able to set goals in keeping with your ability. Confidence works for you in a very positive way, allowing you to move freely without restriction or fear. You know generally what you can and cannot do, and will not attempt something just to bolster your ego. You don't have to, you are already self-confident.

Simple direct strokes indicate objectivity and lack of pretense. You don't feel you have to explain every action. Capital letters are large, which show assurance when beginning something new. You do not decorate or underline your signature, for you have no need to prove yourself to anyone. Your writing style is independently individual, for you also don't apologize for your talents.

SELF-CONFIDENCE

Thanks for your confidence. I'll do a good job for you.

If you are impatient you are always in a hurry to be someplace, you arrive in a rush, and before you've gotten very much out of being there, you're off to the next place. You have a restless nature which suffers a nagging feeling of always being on the verge of missing out on something. You avoid details and routine because they delay you from getting to those exciting experiences that are bound to happen.

The handwriting shows quick, incomplete *t* crossings and haphazardly placed punctuation marks. There is an anxious broadening of the left-hand margin. Terminal letters to words will be unfinished.

IMPATIENCE

We spent r days touring Italy, Spain, France, Portugal and then arrived in north Africa.

The child writes with a pencil because he can erase mistakes. The adult writes with a pencil for the same reason, though he may no longer erase. If you have developed into a cautious person, you avoid bumping into things. One line of handwriting will not bump into the line which follows. The lower loops of the first line will be avoided when writing the second line. If you are feeling your way in the dark, you stretch your hand out to avoid a collision and to separate your body from any invisible object. The frequent use of dashes in your writing accomplishes the same purpose. You are putting greater distance between you and the person to whom you are writing, just as a precaution.

CAUTION

Happy to meet with you — soon. Perhaps tomorrow —? If not — by the end of

The procrastinator's motto is "don't do today what you can put off until tomorrow." Though your intention may be sincere, you rarely finish most things you start out to do. More often than not, you really don't want to do them at all. The initial appeal fades and with it your desire to follow through; therefore, you are forever finding reasons for not being able to get to it.

Stalling is shown in the *t* bar crossing. It starts at the left of the bar and does not follow through. Note also the lack of following through with ending letters of words.

PROCRASTINATION

Tell my secretary to remind me about it tomorrow.

Lying, distorting the truth, and intentionally misrepresenting are factors of deceit. If you are in the habit of doing any one of these things, you earn the characteristic trait of deceitfulness.

The handwriting clues are distortion and misrepresenting of the letter forms. This is very much different from creatively designed and individually styled letters, and should not be confused with the distinctive characteristics of deceit. A dishonest person will try to convince you of his sincerity by giving you something which on the surface resembles what he originally promised, but he knows it does not have the same value. Compulsive deceit shows in the devious routes of letter movements in the samples below. Many are complete reversals of direction. Some of the *o*'s and *a*'s have contrived gaps, indicating the writer is leaving something out intentionally. The two examples cited here show the trait of deceit of two different people.

DECEIT: SIXTEEN-YEAR-OLD MALE STUDENT

sky is falling and I must go above

DECEIT: FORTY-YEAR-OLD MALE DIRECTOR OF A WELFARE PROJECT

problems have been overcome Thanks

You are honest if you have developed the habit of being frank and sincere in your attitudes and behavior. You use the direct approach with people in situations of work and play, presenting yourself as what you believe you are. You make no attempt to cover up shortcomings or devolve blame upon others for your inadequacies and misdeeds. When a situation calls for you to tell an untruth, you are unconvincing, because it is not your normal behavior and you show the discomfort which gives you away. Inexperience and feelings of guilt make you a poor liar. You are happy with your honesty.

Honest writing is simply stated. Letters follow the intended movement of their character, without ornaments to distract and confuse. All marks necessary to the writing structure are present.

HONESTY

Since you ask, you do look more like his mother than his wife.

Summary of Your Social Traits

Indicate below the characteristics which you have found in your handwriting:

___ Extrovert	___ Optimistic
___ Introvert	___ Pessimistic
___ Moral	___ Shy
___ Amoral	___ Ostentatious
___ Generous	___ Procrastinator
___ Conservative	___ Ambitious
___ Frugal	___ Lazy
___ Humorous	___ Proud
___ Witty	___ Vain
___ Sarcastic	___ Humble
___ Stubborn	___ Self-Confident
___ Yielding	___ Impatient
___ Resentful	___ Cautious
___ Compassionate	___ Deceitful
___ Inconsiderate	___ Honest

When you go back to the questionnaire for this chapter (pages 76-77), you may find yourself reconsidering your first reactions.

6.

are you repressed?

The following characteristics are not by themselves signs of suppression or repression. Sometimes they prove to be highly valuable traits when combined with other qualities. This chapter will reveal when they are considered negative to your personality, but before you proceed, complete this questionnaire as best you can.

Yes   No   ?

—   —   —   1. Are you in the habit of daydreaming?

—   —   —   2. Does your mind exaggerate what it sees, hears, and feels?

—   —   —   3. Are you absentminded about things you intended to do, things you said, and promises you made?

—   —   —   4. Do you have the ability to block people from your mind when you want to?

—   —   —   5. Do you spend much time reminiscing about the past?

Yes   No   ?

——   ——   ——   6. Do you dwell on thoughts of death and morbidity?

——   ——   ——   7. Can you accept your weaknesses and still like
yourself?

——   ——   ——   8. Do you have a vivid memory of your childhood frustrations and unpleasant experiences?

——   ——   ——   9. Do you look forward to the future?

——   ——   ——   10. Are you afraid of growing older and what lies
ahead for you?

To answer the question, are you repressed?, honestly, you must
look at yourself with deep introspection. Are you free to express what
dwells within you? Are you feeling and enjoying outwardly all that
you are capable of, and realizing your true potential? Do all your
inner forces work toward adjusting your needs to the outside environment, giving you outlets for self-expression? You are a rare individual
if you can answer affirmatively to these questions, living the perfect
existence seemingly intended for a human being. To be aware and
comfortable with what you are is the greatest assurance of enjoying
life and succeeding in goals, for you have made friends with your
greatest potential enemy—yourself.

Repression is a word frequently referred to in the field of psychology. It is a dangerous foe that works in the dark corners of your
mind, imprisoning desires, fears, and memories from your consciousness so that you are unaware they exist.

A classic example of repression is found in the story of Dr. Jekyll
and Mr. Hyde, by Robert Louis Stevenson. There is, of course, a
moral to the story. It might be embarrassing to uncover your "Hyde,"
but it's more comfortable in the long run than sitting on it all the
time. Failure to recognize and accept what is unpleasant will not remove its presence. You can push it far back into the unconscious,
but memory traces will find an escape hatch or make one by creating
explosions. These explosions are damaging, for they appear in the
form of migraine headaches, high blood pressure, ulcers, skin disorders, overweight and underweight, and mental illness.

Freud and Breuer, in their *Studies on Hysteria,* cite a number
of cases where repression resulted in paralysis, blindness, and im-

potence. Their method of treating patients was first to uncover the repression causing the illness and then have the patient recognize and accept it.

We all have the power to generate light into the dark areas of our minds and to see what is stored there from the past. What you discover might be alarming at first, but you can only conquer an enemy when you know who he is. Negative traits can be reshaped and transformed into positive ones, or they can be completely removed, modified, or adjusted to. Any of these actions would help alleviate the burden which is robbing you of inner freedom.

Once the shackles of repression are cast off, this wasteful energy will be replaced with useful energy, for relieved of this weight you will gain the enthusiasm you lost. The abilities and talents for making life more satisfying can more easily be expressed, and you may be surprised to discover a new potential in you. It is exciting to find something new about ourselves at any stage in life. A man of eighty was asked why, at his age, he was just beginning to undertake a comprehensive study of Latin. He answered, "Because it's the only age I have."

If you can remove some of the blinders and other defense mechanisms, you will be able to move further and faster toward self-actualization. You will also increase the value of what you have to offer others, making it everybody's gain.

We are all subject to moments of illusion and fantasy, which sprinkle our sometimes dull existence with romance and sensation. We come back to earth soon enough, and perhaps bring some of this fantasy into our real world. Creative people operate on both levels, but if they are productive they distinguish between fantasy and reality and have them under control. But fantasizing can be a sign of repression. The danger sets in when fantasy begins to dominate the real existence. Lofty thoughts and imagination can lift you high into the ionosphere. If you remain there too long it will begin to appear real, and you will become so familiar and comfortable with these surroundings that returning to earth will be difficult.

When you begin to move further away from actual living experiences into another dimension of your own creation, truth and fantasy become fused and undistinguishable. Imagined happenings may grow poignant in the memory and real experiences fade into nonexistence.

Imagination may be fanciful and produce images which don't actually exist, but quite frequently it has the wonderful quality of transforming a mental thought into a picture and being able to develop further on real ideas. The upper loops of the handwriting are full and round, giving the mental zone lots of room for thought.

EXAGGERATED IMAGINATION

I can make a million dollars with this idea.

Fantasy carries you away from the basic movement of the letter formations into other shapes and areas of space. The writer identifies in his particular way with what he is writing.

FANTASY

The tree bled as the axe struck.

Fantasy often produces feelings of euphoria and allows you freedom to move into another sphere of thought and emotion. It may also produce feelings of horror if your flight is into a sphere of fear and morbidity. This is indicated by triangular deviations in the letter forms, which show the presence of tension and aggressive action. Heavy pressure, in this context, demonstrates fear and horror.

MORBID FANTASY

Every beast is hungry for devouring Me.

In daydreaming the mind wanders away from its course to some other memory or thought. The habit of daydreaming develops because it is more pleasing than what is really happening. It may not be a serious habit, if controlled, but when it gets out of hand and begins to occur on its own, it interferes with the total personality performance and becomes a handicap. Concentration, time, and effort are wasted with the interruption of a daydream, for you stop what you had been doing and must begin again. Even more dangerous, you might continue mechanically to do something you had not intended.

Retracing letters is a sign of dawdling, that your attention is somewhere else. If you are in the habit of retracing circular forms, the thoughts you are having are pleasant.

DAYDREAMING

Of course I love you, Clark, — I mean, Fred.

People become absentminded about things they would like to forget. The habit stems from lack of desire and interest, but since the personality does not wish to accept this as the cause, the habit is allowed to impose itself indiscriminately, and you become upset about forgetting the things you really want to remember to do.

A word written again after just having completed it, an *a* with a *d* stem, uncrossed *t*'s and undotted *i*'s are all indications of this trait. The repeating of a word after just having been written is more conclusive evidence.

ABSENTMINDEDNESS

I bought the the wood but I forgot to to get nails.

You cancel out many things in your life without any regret or emotional trauma. A project, a friendship, bad feelings, and even ideas can be canceled without fear that they are being repressed, as long as the canceling is a conscious action. However, when you destroy something without knowing why, it is a sign that some associated memory is being repressed. How many people have you met and immediately disliked, without being able to put your finger on the reason? Have you examined why some things which please most people do not please you? When you cancel without conscious reason, you are destroying potential feelings and pleasures which could be enjoyable. The answers are in your memory bank and available for recall.

This sample demonstrates how strokes can cancel out other letters and even complete words by running a line clear through them. This is frequently seen in a signature where the writer has canceled himself out.

CANCELING OUT

You may often ask yourself why you don't do the things you would like to do, and then attribute your inaction to morality or lack of time, money, and opportunity. Any of these reasons may be true, but if your handwriting is similar to the sample below, the real reason is because you are suppressed. Throughout the developing years, you have allowed yourself little freedom for self-expression, confining yourself to limited areas where broad movements are impossible. You have closed yourself into small spaces for so long that the prospect of moving into untested areas now is frightening to you.

Letters are narrow and close together. The writing may be large in height or small, but the space in the loops and between letters and words is suppressed.

SUPPRESSION

When the signs for suppression and canceling out appear together, there is evidence of a strong emotional problem. The writer is unhappily confined by his own inner forces and strikes out against himself in rejection. Tense and despondent, he is his own worst enemy.

SUPPRESSION AND CANCELING OUT

Why do I stay here? Please tell me what to do.

Mary Smith

Nostalgia offers happy moments, and drawing on past experience is a valuable aid for present planning and projecting for the future. However, if you linger too long in memory of the past, you cannot move with a normal pace in a forward direction.

There are numerous reasons for dwelling in the past. It may have been more pleasant then, or even if it were not, the memory that it was pleasant draws you back there again. Another reason may be the fear of facing what lies before you. The future can look ominous in many ways. Aged people sometimes become senile and act childishly. Reduced brain cell replacement and loss of blood and oxygen to the brain are certainly significant factors, but the fear of aging is also a contributing cause for regressing to the past. A feeling of hopelessness for the future may impel one to seek refuge in his past. Children will often behave younger than their years because they don't want to grow up. They want the more exclusive attention they used to receive and are afraid of the added responsibilities expected of them as they grow older. There is often a strong similarity between a child and an aged person with regard to regression. Both want the security of being taken care of by others and the attention that accompanies it.

There are varying degrees of returning to the past. Brief visits to bygone days are normal for all of us. In fact, it can serve to help us measure our growth and make more vivid our life history. But there is a broad range from occasional flights into the past to extreme seclusion into yesterday.

This is the writing of a future-minded individual who takes short trips into the past. The slant moves in a forward direction as well as the crossing of the *t*'s. However, notice the placement of the *i* dots and how they pull back behind the stem of the letter. Since the letter *i* is also a word by itself, meaning the self, the trips the writer takes are very personal and he journeys there alone.

Sorry, I was just thinking of something.

In the writing below there is a conflict and ambivalence toward past and future. The writer is consciously motivated toward the future, but uncontrollable forces keep pulling him back. This action is compulsive and it creates a strain on the personality, for it is like racing forward to meet an objective while an invisible chain keeps jerking him back.

The *i* dots and *t* bar crossings all pull behind the vertical stroke. Future-minded, but something out there is frightening.

Why can't I finish this project? What's holding me up.?

There are primarily two personalities who use the past as a habitat and fall into a conditioned pattern of simulating past experiences as a way of life. The first is one who resisted growing up. Always wanting to remain a child and to be treated like one, he never emotionally accepts or develops maturing attitudes. Whatever his childhood held for him guides his present behavior, though he may have learned how to cover it up on the surface. Throwing tantrums when things don't go his way, playfully mischievous, expecting reward or punishment for his acts, and not accepting the responsibility due at his age level are signs of still remaining in the earlier period of life.

In lingering childhood the middle-zone writing is childishly large. The slant is upright to backward, and the right-hand margin broadens as the left-hand margin narrows.

LINGERING CHILDHOOD

My wife let's me play cards one night a week, but she thinks I'm working Saturday afternoons.

The second is one who has reached maturity on many levels but does not wish to keep pace with the outside environment, so he draws back into himself, and as the world moves forward, he remains in the past. Withdrawn and self-involved, he is a prisoner to the limits of his own world. He may be sufficiently perceptive to realize that some liaison with the outside surroundings is necessary to his survival, and he must be able to relate to others in a limited way.

The handwriting reflects the personal style of the writer, but the slant is backward in the withdrawing position. Dots and other punctuations are behind their proper place, as well as *t* stroke crossings. Margins narrow at the left and broaden at the right.

MATURE WITHDRAWAL

I was always my father's favorite, but I know now he really didn't care because he left me when I was ten and never came back.

Here is an example of a way-out individual, completely lost from reality and living in a world which he created from past experiences of fantasy and illusion. His vivid imagination and undeniable creative talent are used to help him escape. Actively occupied in this world, he is busy applying his skills to planning and building on his ideas. He may be extremely intelligent and well organized, but his thinking is far removed from the living society. He is both the sole inhabitant and dictator of this domain, encountering no competition.

CREATIVE WITHDRAWAL

My ship leaves for Mars at 4:00

Characteristics of Repression

At times it is tempting to live in a private world of our own, removing the presence of other people, the struggles and hardships of daily life, and be able to take flight into a world we create, where we control the outcome. Who can judge from another individual which is the happier world? It is presumed to be against nature's plan for man to live in isolation, for it is proven that all species of life survive only in groups. We can only hope that the individual need to identify with other human beings is strong enough to overcome the temptation to destroy the world outside himself for a limited but safe existence.

If sufficiently motivated toward greater self-realization, you will be able to identify readily the characteristics which apply to you:

___ Exaggerated imagination   ___ Suppression and canceling

___ Fantasizing   ___ Occasional reveries

___ Morbid fantasizing   ___ Conflict of past and future

___ Daydreaming   ___ Living in the past

___ Absentmindedness   (child ___   adult ___)

___ Canceling out   ___ Creative withdrawal

___ Suppression

7.

your talent potential

Listed below are fields for creative expression. Indicate whether you believe yourself capable of expressing yourself in any of these areas. The criteria are not based on past experience of success and failure, or ever having exposed yourself to these endeavors. Answer "Yes" if you think you have a talent which could be developed.

Yes	No	?	
___	___	___	1. Art
___	___	___	2. Dance
___	___	___	3. Music
___	___	___	4. Creative writing
___	___	___	5. Acting
___	___	___	6. Science
___	___	___	7. Architecture
___	___	___	8. Leadership/Organization
___	___	___	9. Philosophy
___	___	___	10. Spiritual leadership

You may never in your entire lifetime pursue certain objectives because you do not believe you have the talent and ability to be successful in them. Yet all creatively productive people will readily submit to the rigors of discipline and training they must endure before enjoying the satisfaction of their talent. Whether or not you decide to devote energy and time at this stage of your life in an artistic pursuit, you should know what innate abilities you possess, for they can afford you added pleasure.

If you never attempt anything for the first time and give it a real try, you will really never know whether or not you can do it. Talent which remains dormant and unexpressed is meaningless. Your handwriting may reveal qualities which in combination with each other indicate a disposition to a particular or uncommon ability. If you stir these qualities with desire, they will find a way to express an outward talent. Strong desire is the most essential ingredient for bringing forth a talent, because it sustains the will and determination to make it grow.

Desire, without natural ability, would lead to nothing more than mediocrity, regardless of all the enthusiasm and effort expended. Though it isn't necessary to excel in something in order to enjoy it for one's private pleasure, it must be a natural ability to prove a real talent. Characteristics for various talents may interrelate or they may vary, depending upon what is called for in the particular field of expression. For example, a neurosurgeon requires good motor coordination and manipulative skill, a psychiatrist does not. The scientist deals with facts and truths, the artist with abstract images. One good quality can inhibit or conflict with another good quality when they are both applied to one purpose; therefore, the scientist and the artist may see things differently. A particular talent is developed by the strength of the qualities essential to it.

The following general categories describe the characteristics needed for a type of talent. You, undoubtedly, fit into one of them, and it is hoped that it has some advantage in your present life. If not, think on it, and weigh it against the present apportionment of your time. You may conclude that it isn't too late to give it a go.

ARTIST

An eye for color, form, and composition is a basic tool of the artist. Though art forms have changed in different periods of history, and may continue to do so, the principle of color, form, and composition will always remain an important criterion for good artwork.

Color is shown in handwriting by the contrast of light and dark in the letter strokes. Form is represented by variation of letter shapes, and composition in the placement of shapes and the overall design of the writing.

The most significant characteristic discernible for art potential is the freedom the writer uses when breaking into space. The movement may be gracefully conforming or abstracted, depending upon individual style, but liberties are taken to enhance the entire design.

GRACEFUL

A thing of beauty is a joy forever;

ABSTRACTED

Painting is a very personal expression.

DANCER

A good sense of rhythm, timing, and coordination is necessary to the dance form. Though all parts of the body are used in the dancing movement, the greatest concentration is placed upon the arms and legs. The feeling for dance will show in the writer's rhythmical swing of letter connections (arms) and lower loops with syncopated emphasis on *i* dots and punctuation marks. Note that the middle zone of writing is relatively small, as well as the upper zone (head). The dancer is most concerned with leg and arm movements.

When the band begins to play, I sway.

MUSICIAN

The natural ability of a musician is a good ear for sound, a feeling for pacing and phrasing, and a sympathetic understanding of the instruments of the body in playing the music. Music has many of the characteristics of art and dance. The noted modern painter, Paul Klee, was also a musician. He transposed onto canvas many patterns of musical progression which reflected delightful and humorous rhythms. However, with the musician, sound dominates over vision. Even after his deafness, Beethoven was able to compose with his mind's ear which still carried a long range of sound memories.

If you are more perceptive to sound than you are to what you see, and learn more readily by listening than by looking, you are considered ear minded. When someone speaks, you turn your eyes away from him to concentrate on what is being said. When listening to music, you close your eyes to cut off visual distractions. The musician may be looking at music or writing it, but he predominantly hears it.

The writing moves rhythmically across the page, one stroke leading to the next, even connecting words together. Intervals between letters and words are evenly spaced. Loud and soft sounds are denoted by alternating light and dark strokes, with a punctuated emphasis of dots, periods, and apostrophes.

She will play the third movement!

CREATIVE WRITER

To prove your writing ability you must be able to collect your thoughts, imagination, and knowledge and organize them into a workable central theme to be expressed in words. Your mind dwells in the high atmosphere of thought, which is continually fed by impressions of the things you see, hear, and feel. You are open-minded and suggestible, as indicated by the *a* and *o* openings. You have a good ability to concentrate, shown by small middle-zone letters. You reach high for new ideas or situations as seen by a high upper zone, *t* crossings, and punctuation. Through association with literature, you may use printed letters and other literary marks in the handwriting.

In the old dusty oaken chair, elegantly sat a black cat.

Each talent can be expressed in more than one way. For example, if you show an inclination toward creative writing, have a quick and penetrating mind, and also possess the social characteristic wit, you could also be a satirist, humorist, or literary critic.

If you have a knack for art, with the kind of mind which is more evaluative than emotional, disciplined, with good concentration ability, you are more a candidate for commercial aspects of art. Fine arts require more liberalism and less orthodoxy after the basic principles are learned and applied.

When you evaluate your other characteristics, previously described so far, you will be able to determine realistic avenues for your natural talents.

THE ACTOR

A fine actor can project himself into the role of another. He identifies something in himself with the person he portrays so that he might be convincing to himself as well as the audience. Sympathetic and understanding, he likes people and responds to them no matter what outward image he may project. Exceptional actors like Helen Hayes, Frederic March, John Mills, and Judith Anderson are assuming and natural when they appear in public, showing that they are comfortable with their true personalities.

There are very few identifiable characteristics of the actor in the handwriting, for the same qualities could easily be transferred to other dynamic fields of expression. He has strong emotions, will, and determination and the inner freedom to use them. Most actors reflect this in their forward heavy slant and free use of space when writing.

I like portraying real characters.

SCIENTIST

Science deals with truths and facts. Discoveries are founded on concrete principles and tested to establish their true value. The scientific mind searches for answers without discarding a single minute clue, for it might prove valuable. One seemingly small problem is often the study of a lifetime, with many people devoting themselves to it.

The handwriting shows an exceptional ability to concentrate by the very small legibly written letters. Direct and simple strokes show an organized type of thinking, unconfused by superficial decorations. The writing is carefully punctuated, indicating attention to details. Objectivity is seen in the upright slant, and the general pattern of writing is efficient and unemotional.

The eighteen amino acids have been recognized in similian form in the meteorite which a short time ago fell to the earth in Australia.

ARCHITECT

A structure requires a solid base, so that whatever is built upon it does not collapse. A sense of design and an understanding of the use of space are the builder's basic tools. Imagination and daring are the qualities which distinguish one architect from another, but all must be able to serve the purposes of the intended structure. An artist wants his studio built to receive the northern light, a concert hall must be constructed with good acoustics, the number of rooms available for profit must be considered in the design of office buildings and hotels, shopping centers are built in large or growing communities and must provide accessible parking space, and so on. The builder is ever alerted not only to present serviceability, but also the prospects to how it will serve in the future.

The handwriting shows a strong and even base line, indicating that the writing stands on secure ground. The tops of middle-zone letters tends to be broad and flat, clearly recognizable in the small letter *r*. The writing is clear and well organized. An architect may be emotional, but his emotions are under control as indicated by the even height of the middle-zone letters.

The roof of the glass window rooms will be more heavily insulated to reduce the heat.

LEADER—ORGANIZER OF PEOPLE

Sales managers, public officials, club leaders, union bosses, heads of liberal movements, evangelists, reformers, and those in a position to influence and lead people have a number of characteristics in common with each other. They look for attention and recognition; therefore, the handwriting is large, dominating the paper. They are future-minded and generally extroverts, causing a forward slant in writing direction. Strongly motivated to action, the strokes are heavy in pressure and long in determination.

A leader, to hold onto his position, shows firmness of purpose. He is not easily sidetracked or vulnerable to influence; therefore, connecting strokes are rigid and ending strokes blunt. A true leader carries the burden of responsibility on his own shoulders; therefore, he is strong-willed and adamant about the position he takes. This is demonstrated by long and heavy *t* bar crossings and straight, thick, lower loop strokes. A final, but very important trait, is that this individual is high goal oriented. The *t* bar crossings are high and sometimes above the stem with an upward-moving slant. For others, this striving may be far-reaching and unrealistic, but this dynamic personality believes . . . "But a man's reach should exceed his grasp, Or what's a heaven for?"

I most humbly accept your nomination

PHILOSOPHER

There are as many different philosophies as there are men who have founded them. Pythagoras was concerned with mathematical demonstration and deduction, and he combined rational science with mysticism. Socrates was most concerned with the truth of man's existence and his beliefs were based on moral values. Thomas Aquinas was the leading philosopher of the Roman Catholic Church. He submitted philosophy to theology. Nietzsche was a psychological philosopher involved with unmasking hypocrisy and exposing delusions and perverted judgment. He attempted to pave the way for man to transform into a high type—the superman.

All forms of philosophy deal with higher thought and extrapolation, and all are in search of a truth to live by. The philosophical mind is moral to his system of principles and views. The handwriting pressure is light, showing sensitivity to the use of all things. Strokes reach high up into the mental zone, where most of the energy and time are spent, leaving the lower physical zone understated. Dots and other punctuation marks are loftily placed and not confined to the center social zone. Capitals and beginning letters of words stand out much larger than the other writing, like accentuated thoughts. Concentration and mental discipline are observed in the small, clearly defined middle-zone characters.

No thought is pure when it is poisoned with desire.

SPIRITUAL LEADER

There are many similarities in the handwriting of the philosophical mind and that of a person with a religious calling. Both tend to reject materialism, seeking gratification in revelations and in service to humanity and God (one or the other, or both). The difference is the rigidity with which the spiritual leader follows theistic doctrines and adherence to the moral obligations stemming from his beliefs. He is committed to abide strictly to the tenets of his religion, though interpretation may give some leeway.

Upper loop letters reach high into the heavenly sphere, while the physical lower loops are short and unimportant. Letters are written lightly with a sensitive touch. Though many high flourishes may appear, *i* dots are placed responsibly directly over the *i* stem.

Tradition and conformance to an unchanging belief are noted in the idealized but still conventional capital letters. Religious symbolism often appears in the form of the *t* resembling the holy cross, and perhaps a flourish stroke will extend far over the small letters like a shelter from above protecting the flock below.

There is no questioning the wisdom of the Lord and His laws for mankind.

Talent Potential Evaluation

You may possess a particular talent, included in this chapter, which doesn't comply with the handwriting indices. This chapter is just to alert you that, if the signs do appear in your handwriting, you have the qualities more conducive to the talent described, and to give you the opportunity to look more closely at it.

Indicate below any potential talents you have discovered by analyzing your handwriting.

___ Art   ___ Science
___ Dance   ___ Architecture
___ Music   ___ Leadership/Organization
___ Creative writing   ___ Philosophy
___ Acting   ___ Spiritual leadership

8.

awareness of physical problems

You may not always be consciously aware that some physical problem is disturbing you. The desire to ignore it may be so strong that it is blocked from your mind. Quite frequently a physical problem appears in the handwriting, like a cry from the unconscious to warn you that something is wrong.

List below any general ailments which you are aware of that are present in the parts of the body indicated.

Yes	No	?	
___	___	___	1. Head and neck_____
___	___	___	2. Trunk _____
___	___	___	3. Legs and feet_____
___	___	___	4. Arms and hands_____
___	___	___	5. Nervous system_____

Yes   No   ?

——— ——— ———   6. Motor disturbance——————————————————

——— ——— ———   7. Fatiguing illness——————————————————

It is hoped that if you encounter the presence of a physical problem in your handwriting, which you did not know before, you will not become alarmed but will see a physician for qualified diagnosis and attention.

It is not a new theory that your lower level of consciousness is in touch with all parts of the body and their functions. When in distress, the malfunctioning part signals a message to the brain. If unhampered by psychological barriers, the brain will telegraph its special agents assigned to that location to try to alleviate the trouble.

Recent studies of the brain's control over the body have shown some remarkable results. An American experimental clinic demonstrated a man's ability to reduce his own blood pressure by sheer willpower. No medication or apparatus was used, except a bed and the equipment needed to register the changes in his pressure. A clinic enclosed a yogi in a sealed chamber, slowly reducing the amount of oxygen fed into it until there was so little that ordinarily no human being could still stay alive. He remained in this state for several hours, returning to his former condition without sustaining any damage.

Physical problems generally make themselves known to us by means of pains and aches, and with a little searching we can usually determine the source. Living excesses often cause ulcers, high blood pressure, insomnia, nervous tension, and headaches, and we know it's time to start taking things a little easier. However, the physical disturbances which are outwardly ignored sometimes show up in the handwriting to reveal that they do bother you.

Freud studied many people suffering from hysterical illnesses. There was nothing physically wrong with the patients, yet they suffered all the pains and symptoms of real illness. In many such cases unconscious memory associations, together with guilt and anxiety, produced illnesses which were cured after the patient recognized and accepted what brought them on in the first place. A young girl's blindness was lifted after she was able to face the true circumstances of her father's death. She had been forced to identify his body as it lay naked on a bed in a house of prostitution. The memory was so horrifying that she blocked it from her vision by becoming blind. Another case was that of a child suffering from convulsions due to a lost memory of a terrible fear when a wild dog chased her. A theoretical explanation for this is that the nervous system becomes overstimulated and releases surplus energy to the parts of the body involved in the incident of excitability. According to this theory, it would seem that the more sensitively excitable a person you are, the more you are prone to psychosomatic disturbances.

When you were a child, first learning to write in the three zonal areas, the letter form was presented like a human body. Even if the teacher did not demonstrate this method, you would have made the natural association of the upper zone as the head, the middle zone as the body, and the lower zone as the legs. When you moved on to cursive writing, you visualized the letter connections as arms swinging along. These associations are retained throughout your life when writing though you are no longer consciously aware of them.

When a part of your body is in distress, it may communicate this in the same corresponding place of the letter body like a mirrored image. A deviation from the natural letter formation will occur with sufficient frequency to rule out any coincidence.

Head Pain (Neck Included).   Small arrow-like projections indicate a point of tension. The writing has turned from its normal course in this particular place because it unconsciously meets with an obstacle.

I have a throbbing headache.

When pain is not predominant, but there is some loss in sight, hearing, memory, or nerve damage, this may be demonstrated in the writing by small gaps or considerable lightening of the upper part of the stroke. It says that something is missing or not functioning.

LOSS IN HEAD AREA

I lost my right eye thirty years ago.

Center Body Trouble. The thorax and abdomen are represented by the middle-zone letters (the small characters). Evidence
of trouble in this area is indicated the same way as described above,
by stopping points which jut out from the normal movement of the
stroke, or by lifting the pen to make deliberate gaps or lightened
areas. To be significant, these idiosyncrasies of movement must appear a number of times in the writing—otherwise it could be due to
an accident or a faulty writing tool.

PAIN

Maybe I'm suffering with an ulcer.

LOSS

I just had a hysterectomy.

Legs and Feet. The lower portion of the body is considered
the greatest distributor of physical energy. It holds the weight of the
other parts and transports them from place to place. The lower zone
of writing is correspondingly called the physical zone. The sample
below is the writing of a man who had received a shrapnel wound in
World War II in his left leg, and has been limping on it ever since.
He not only lightens the pressure but also leaves gaps in the area
representing the injury he sustained, the left side of the lower loops.
When questioned, he stated that he was totally unaware of this phenomenon in his writing, and that having lived so long with this limp
without pain he was almost unconscious of it.

LEFT LEG LIMP

*I've listened closely to you speaking for
one nice long evening.*

Arms and Hands. Strokes which begin a word, connect two
letters, or end a word in the middle zone of writing represent the arms
and hands. If the writing hand is experiencing pain, naturally the

entire writing pattern will be affected and inadequate for qualified analysis. However, there are problems in this area which do not disturb the actual writing process, and they appear in the places described.

PAIN

Football was a favorite childhood sport!

LOSS

D. of two fingers caught in the grinder.

Nervous Disorders. When nervous problems exist, balance and coordination of the entire body system are thrown out of gear. Letters are corrugated and the base line is uneven, showing loss of control. Pressure may be light or heavy, depending upon other facets of the personality, but a general instability will be noted in the overall writing pattern. Speed of writing is slower than the writer's normal pace because nervous stress impedes the flow of movement even in the fast writer.

Extreme tension is often indicated by the pen exerting additional pressure during the interval of writing. This added pressure causes more ink to flow from the pen, creating little blobs or dots along the outline of the letter.

GENERAL NERVOUS CONDITION

I have been jumpy all day today.

EXTREME TENSION

We have a two weeks deadline.

Psychomotor Problems. When the brain and sensory system do not respond to each other with adequate timing and rapport, unsure and awkward physical actions occur. Motor problems involving speech, hearing, vision, or body movements carry over to the handwriting in the form of slow and labored writing. The tracing of letters becomes a difficult task, especially in turning a curve or changing the direction of movement, for the mind and muscles are challenged with a greater demand. This challenge is not met easily by one with motor problems; therefore, stoppage and distorted-looking letter characters result.

People who trip frequently, stutter, misinterpret what they hear, and generally respond slowly and with effort to a self-imposed mental command are often considered by others to be lazy. The cause may be insufficient coordination of the psychomotor system.

POOR COORDINATION

I'm not fast enough to make the team.

Fatiguing Illnesses. Anemia, low blood pressure, malnutrition, and circulatory diseases are a few of the problems which cause dissipation of physical energy. When the writing pressure is inconsistent throughout the entire writing process, beginning strong and too quickly turning weak, it is evident that this is not normal for the writer. He begins a sentence or paragraph with his usual enthusiasm and energy, but, tiring rapidly, the grip on his pen weakens, resulting in lighter strokes. Fatigue will also pull the hand down and the writing line, as energy is required to maintain a stable or uphill line of writing. With every new sentence, the writer attempts to resume his normal intensity of movement, but physically he cannot sustain it.

PHYSICAL FATIGUE

I'm not as productive as I used to be. There was a time I could handle the work of ten men

Evaluation

Graphology should not be used to diagnose specific illnesses, for it isn't the physical body itself which is being examined but only the indications communicated by the person through the handwriting that something is amiss. These clues, whether revealed consciously or unconsciously, should be considered and heeded to. Many people suffer unduly because they prefer to ignore the symptoms of illness for so long that they begin to accept the ailment as a normal condition. If any of these symptoms are observable in your handwriting you might consider how they apply to you and if necessary take steps to correct the situation.

Indicate any observable symptoms below:

___ Head and neck pain   ___ Arms and hands
___ Loss in head area   ___ Nervous disorder
___ Center body problems   ___ Motor disturbance
___ Leg and feet problems   ___ Fatiguing illness

9.

your sexuality

Most people generally evaluate their desires, passions, and sexual performance by what they believe to be the social normal standard. Early indoctrination of what is considered normal sexual behavior by family, friends, physician, and social laws guides us to a position on the yardstick where we measure ourselves in relation to the average. We are sometimes shocked from that position by new surveys, reports, and studies which then cause us to reevaluate how we stand in the social sexual behavior spectrum.

Sexuality begins as a personal need. The first measurement should be how much of that need is fulfilled, redirected into other outlets, or left totally unsatisfied. An individual frustrated by failure to achieve other objectives may overcompensate by increasing his sexual activity. Conversely, someone who is fired by ambition and is successful in worldly pursuits may drain his natural sexual energy, or he may in this way be further feeding his sexual appetite. There are no convenient rules for individual sexual behavior patterns, but we are today aware of the great influence they exert over the total personality.

Yes	No	?	
___	___	___	1. Are you hypersexual?
___	___	___	2. Do you consider yourself undersexed?
___	___	___	3. Have you a normal sexual appetite?
___	___	___	4. Are you performing to your normal capacity?
___	___	___	5. Are you a romantic?
___	___	___	6. Do you enjoy sexual activity?
___	___	___	7. Are you conventional in your attitudes?
___	___	___	8. Do you consciously or unconsciously withdraw?

The only surprises you will encounter in the following pages will be those you learn about yourself. Literature describing the practices and sexual attitudes of other periods and cultures leaves no doubt that there is no new sexual phenomenon which has not before been experienced in the history of man.

When Freud expounded his theories on the sexuality in children, he was laughed at and humiliated. This now seems a strange reaction, for every mother can clearly observe sexual behavior in her child without studying child psychology.

The sexual instinct is born into every living organism for the natural plan of reproduction. Even if the function of procreation is thwarted, the instinct remains. A number of factors influence the sexual behavior of the human being, and it is difficult to determine which factor is the most influential. You are born with certain inherited traits into a social and physical environment, and as a child you don't have too much control over these conditions. You grow sexually along with your total growth, for with the physical feelings and changes are developed sexual attitudes which guide your behavior. The sexual instinct is one of your strongest motivational forces, and with an open mind you can learn a great deal about yourself by examining your sexual attitudes.

If, as a growing child, you had had the intellectual and emotional maturity to understand the sexual development taking place, there would be fewer problems in your adulthood. As a child, you had limited experience to draw from, and had to rely upon guidance from others. And the child is dependent primarily upon the parents for guidance and understanding in these matters. Too frequently, the parents are appalled, humiliated, and even shocked when they discover their child in some form of sexual play. The steps they take often create long-lasting, damaging effects.

The sexual instinct stimulates the body system to produce energy. This energy seeks to be liberated. After childhood, it is difficult to determine whether the glandular system is the first to act, or the senses which stimulate the sexual urge. It is more probable in most cases a closely timed interaction of the two. When you are mentally excited, the energy your body is building up looks for an outlet which closely approximates the cause of excitement. If you do not find some way to unleash this energy, at least in small amounts, it may have one of two damaging effects. It may strain and weaken you both physically and emotionally so that you lose your normal capacity to build up this kind of excitement in the future. The other possible condition is that you hold this excitement inside of you, allowing it to grow to explosive proportions until it finally bursts out in uncontrollable acts. A balloon continuously pumped with air will eventually burst, but if air is occasionally allowed to escape the balloon will remain intact.

A healthy sexual appetite, which seeks gratification by the intended source, is performing a natural function in keeping with the person's individual need. If one partner's requirements do not match his own, he may find it within his moral and ethical boundaries to cohabitate with another or others to satisfy the excess. If the sexual instinct is not strong (unconnected to physical or emotional reasons), there may be a problem in satisfying the needs of a partner, but there is less cause for personal frustration in sex and in setting other goals for achievement. The problem of sufficiently satisfying a mate can be resolved when there is no hang-up relating to a moderate or low sexual appetite. With love, understanding, and patience adjustments can be made for a sexually happy union.

The sexual instinct is the triggering mechanism for building up sexual energy. This source of energy is earmarked for release through sexual activity. The graphological evaluation of your sexuality is based on these factors:

1. The amount of sexual energy generated.
2. The amount actually used for sexual activity.
3. Attitudes toward sex.
4. Sexual repression.

Heredity factors cannot be considered in the graphological analysis because you are observed without benefit of your ancestry and their handwriting. However, since all your emotions come into play in the ultimate sexual expression, there will be enough information to draw from to determine what you are sexually.

You Are Hypersexual.   Long, full, and heavy-pressure downward strokes in the lower zone indicate an excess of physical energy. Sexuality is strong and long lasting, and finds its release in physical expression. Strokes follow through regardless of what might be in the way, just as the intense sexual needs find means to complete satisfaction. The lower zone dominants the total writing pattern, as sexuality dominates the total personality. You linger with pleasure in this lower physical zone.

AGGRESSIVE AND STRONG

PLAYFUL AND STRONG

You Are Strong Sexually.   This is demonstrated by long, enduring lower loops written with heavy pressure. Though you emphasize the lower zonal area, it is not at the sacrifice of your other movements. Sex is an important part of your life to which you devote time and energy, but you still have plenty left over for other objectives.

You Have Moderate Sexuality. Your sexual appetite is curbed and you are more motivated by the pleasure from sexual activity than by intense drive to release physical energy. This is seen in the curved movement of the lower loops. Even though substantial pressure may be exerted, a curve does not carry with it the same force as a straight line. Your sexual needs are in balance with other social-emotional needs, providing the lower loops are approximately two times the length of the middle-zone letters. If they are longer, your imagination exceeds your true need.

Of course, if your mother's home, we'll go out to a movie!

You Are Undersexed. Whether done with awareness or unconsciously, you have cut off the normal supply of energy directed for sexual release. This is characterized in your handwriting by the lower zone practically disappearing. The lower loops are so small and short that they look stunted, as though they had been chopped off. You attempt to compensate by enlarging one of the other two zones, but you can never maintain a happy balance. Children often indicate their sexual timidity and fear in not daring to probe too far into the lower zone.

This aborting of sexual energy is not a normal condition in an adult and should not be ignored. This energy may be going someplace too far removed from the intended outlet to be healthy.

Home and friends are more important than anything or anybody.

Amount of Sexual Energy You Use. You may or may not be using your total sexual strength, and only you can be made aware of whether or not you do. The drive and energy may be working within you, but another force holds you back, so that you do not perform as the complete sexual you.

You may carry out a complete physical action by finishing what you begin with at least the same degree of strength. The lower loop follows through with the same amount of pressure on the upward movement, crossing at the imaginary base line.

COMPLETING THE ACTION

I felt complete relief when the job was done.

Or pressure is lost as the lower loop moves back upward, indicating that all the sexual strength is exerted in the beginning action, with little follow through.

WEAKENING THE ACTION

I get discouraged when she complains

When the lower loop is crossed on the upward movement prematurely, it is a way of finishing the action off quickly. It may give the impression of being complete, but that's just what it's intended to give—an impression.

CUTTING OFF THE ACTION

I can do a good job for you in half the time.

Here there is no attempt to mislead. The writer stops short midway up the lower loop, leaving the unfinished action hanging in midair.

I usually get back to what I began eventually.

You Are a Romantic Lover. As a man, you love the whole concept of woman. As a woman, you appreciate the man who is conscious of you as a woman, and have no difficulty living up to your role. Both of you are aware of yourselves and each other, using your talent of imagination to enhance a pleasurably shared experience. You are sensitive, for when you tune in, you pick up the subtler frequencies of your partner's feelings and responses, which further stimulates and affords you even greater pleasure.

You have attached aesthetic qualities to your sexual expression, which have tempered the urgency for immediate and indiscriminate sex outlets. Your mind is very much a part of the sexual role you play, and though the actual energy expended is not dynamic, the total sexual experience is exceedingly gratifying for both you and your mate.

If you are female, your handwriting shows lighter pressure than the romantic male. Both of you move forward in slant, as you lean toward intimate relationships. The lower loops are long and full, gracefully executed, and they touch other letters intimately. Every movement is relished and ends with the same consideration given throughout the entire movement, seen by the lingering sweep of the lower loop endings.

FEMALE ROMANTIC

I feel your eyes on every part of me, and it makes me tingle.

MALE ROMANTIC

Just stand there without moving - just the sight of you pleases me.

You Are a Sensualist.   In the chapter describing motivation symbols, the circle was represented as the symbol of love. One of the important factors of love, introduced to you quite early in life, is pleasure. A greater capacity and desire for pleasure which seeks its delights in physical sensations is the quality of the sensualist.

Motivated by pure pleasure, the physical zone of your writing is strong and largely circular. You fully enjoy this one area in a free and primitive way, though you may isolate it from other aspects of intellectual thought and attitude. However strong may be your other purposes, you are highly vulnerable to the lure of pleasure.

Pleasure is the only purpose in life.

You Are Sexually Conventional.   You are in control of your sexual behavior, directing your urges and desires to conform to what you believe meets the accepted standards and principles of the society. Sex to you is less personalized and less freely expressed because of these built-in controls. You have rules to abide by and tradition to fall back on.

Your handwriting will reflect a lower zone which is consistently uniform in its standard length, width, and configuration. As your sexual attitudes have not changed, neither have these lower loops deviated from the early learned model. This pattern is efficient, familiar, and comfortable for you, and you continue to conform to what you still believe is proper.

I respect my parents and everything they ever taught me.

You Are Sexually Repressed.   The average person has some inhibitions about his sexuality, which he may be aware of and handle in his own way without a consequent psychosexual trauma. Sexual repression is referred to here as a blocking out of the true needs and desires, so that the sexual energy is forced to find other routes of escape. If the other routes do not satisfy the physical-sexual need, explosions may occur in the way of nervous tension, hostile aggression, and asocial behavior or illness or withdrawal.

The exact route cannot be detected by a handwriting analysis. We can only know that it is not the normal one. The handwriting indications are: (a) the deviated direction of the lower loops, (b) the time spent in making that movement, and (c) the amount of force behind it.

STRONG SEXUALITY EXPRESSED AGGRESSIVELY

I laughed when he filed bancruptcy!

REFUSAL TO FACE SEXUAL REALITIES

Why must we follow what everyone else does?

MILD WITHDRAWAL

I really try to satisfy him, but his so demanding.

AMBIVALENT WITHDRAWAL

If you'll only give me one more chance, you'll

You will note that in each case cited above the lower loop stroke pulls back into the past instead of moving in the natural forward direction, intended to lead you to the next letter form. The farther back the stroke is pulled, the more time and energy are needed to return to the next point of action. You may conclude, therefore, that the greater the length of misdirection of the lower loop, the greater the withdrawal from natural sexual expression.

When this backward-moving stroke is straight and inflexible, it is a further indication that sexual withdrawal is resolute and not easily reversible. Add extreme pressure to these other characteristics and you will find a personality with a high degree of sexuality, self-imposedly repressed.

Your Sexual Expression Evaluation

Indicate below the traits which appear with dominance in your handwriting sample. If there are characteristics in the lower zone of your writing which have not been explained in this chapter, apply the principles of the motivation symbols and their meanings in the earlier part of this book.

This evaluation is highly personal. No one can or should stand in critical judgment, except yourself, and then only with a positive outlook.

___ Hypersexual   ___ Sensualist
___ Strong sexuality   ___ Conventional
___ Moderate sexuality   ___ Sexually repressed
___ Undersexed   Withdrawal ___
___ Total sexual expression   Redirection ___
___ Incomplete sexual expression   Ambivalence ___
___ Romantic

10.

your self-image

___ ___ ___   1. Would you like to be more outgoing than you are?

___ ___ ___   2. Do you try to give the impression of being an introvert, though you are not?

___ ___ ___   3. Do you believe yourself to be aesthetically sensitive?

___ ___ ___   4. Do you try to project this image though you doubt it to be true of you?

___ ___ ___   5. Are you an emotional person who tries to appear cool and reserved?

___ ___ ___   6. Do you hold yourself in higher esteem than others?

___ ___ ___   7. Do you generally hold yourself in less esteem than others?

___ ___ ___   8. Can you mentally block out other people from your existence?

___ ___ ___   9. Are you an individual?

Yes   No   ?

—   —   —   10. Is your family more important to you than yourself?

—   —   —   11. If a woman, do you consider yourself valuable only as a wife and mother?

—   —   —   12. If a woman, do you reject the role of wife?

—   —   —   13. Are you the most important person in the world?

—   —   —   14. Do you try to convince yourself and others of your importance?

—   —   —   15. Are you an egoist, involved only with yourself?

—   —   —   16. Do you have a deflated ego and a small self-image?

—   —   —   17. Do you know who you are and what your purpose is in life?

—   —   —   18. Do you refuse to face the negative characteristics of your personality?

—   —   —   19. Do you often do things to hurt yourself, knowingly or unconsciously?

—   —   —   20. Do you comfortably accept what you believe yourself to be, and move freely and securely in that role?

This is another parlor game you can play at a social gathering, if you wish to lose friends.

One of the most important roles of the psychiatrist, in relating to his patient, is to help him build or restore his self-image. Personalities may outwardly project confidence and love of self, but suffer inwardly with doubts, recriminations, and self-dislike. This person is often unaware that his ego may be weak, for he compensates with superficial rewards fed by the people around him, so that he may come through to them and himself as assured and in command. An obvious example is the person who protests too much. His desperation to convince often indicates his shaky position. People who criticize and judge others are frequently setting up guards against their own vulnerabilities.

If you are truly a modest and shy individual, you may be grossly underrating your value to yourself and others and, consequently, not enjoying the most that's in you.

In this chapter you will have an opportunity to measure what you have always thought yourself to be to yourself and others, with the new attitudes or insight gained from this self-analysis. A positive aim is a comfortable acceptance of what you are now, what you are capable of being in the future, and a decision in your best interest of how to move between the two.

ARE YOU THE PERSON YOU WANT OTHERS TO THINK YOU ARE?

Your signature is the clue which reveals if you are the person you try to appear to be to others. If you have not signed your full signature to your letter sample, do so now in your usual style before continuing to read further. A signature should only be analyzed with the message written before it, for the differences between the two are highly significant.

The body of the writing is you, the signature is the image you wish to project to others. If the pattern and emphasis of both are the same, you are presenting yourself exactly as you are.

People feel that standing up amidst a seated crowd is a sign of aggressiveness. If you wish to appear more aggressive than you are, the capital letters of your signature will be substantially larger than in the other writing. You don't really feel so bold, but you want others not to see you as timid.

DESIRE TO APPEAR MORE AGGRESSIVE

All I can say is Thank you This has been an honor J. J. Smith

If your concept of beauty and design appear only in your signature, you are only concerned with conveying an impression to others, with no true feeling for the aesthetic. You wish to appear attractive and romantic, but you do not find these qualities within yourself.

PROJECTING ARTISTIC IMAGE

The Opera was delightful Thanks for inviting me Loraine Fields

You assume a modest pose, reducing yourself to others, yet satisfied that you are much more. You seek excuses and apologize to others for your talent and ability, all the while secure in what you think of yourself.

HYPOCRITICAL MODESTY

I'll be happy to serve in whatever way I can. Sam Richards

When you underscore your signature, you are adding an extra effort to make it stand out from its surroundings and emphasize its importance. It is like wanting to stand out in a crowd.

EMPHASIZING YOUR IMPORTANCE

I'll consider your proposal & let you know! Arthur Buxley

The last stroke of your name is drawn out because you feel it is an understatement of what you are. There is more . . . and more . . . and more. . . .

MORE TO YOU THAN JUST A NAME

.. and I'd like us to get to know one another better Claire Anderson

You may not be as busy a person as you pretend, if the body of your writing is executed at a much slower rate of speed than your signature, which is a reflection of your true pace of action.

SHOWING YOURSELF AS BUSY AND ACTIVE

As soon as I have time, I promise to ring you.   John Flanger

Your writing slant is upright, indicating a cool and impersonal attitude. Your signature attempts to convey the opposite.

EXTENDING EMOTIONS YOU DON'T FEEL

I wish you all the happiness in the world.   Uncle Milton

The signature slant belies the warm, outgoing person you actually are. If only the written signature were observed, you would graphologically be considered an unemotive individual, which is not true of you.

ATTEMPT TO APPEAR RESERVED, BUT EMOTIONAL

Your apology isn't necessary. I understand your position.   Lawrence Pearson

COMPARING YOURSELF TO OTHERS

You have feelings about the person to whom you are writing, and they are always in relation to yourself in some way. When alerted to the handwriting indications, your feeling about the person becomes almost obvious. The most discernible clues are found in your writing of their name, as this conveys what you actually think of them.

When you think little of someone, his or her image is reduced in your mind and correspondingly reduced when writing the name. If you were embarrassed or thought little of a companion you were forced to introduce to someone else, you would present her or him meekly and try to minimize that person's presence.

LOW OPINION OF THE OTHER PERSON

Dear Mr. Gillin:
Your bid does not meet the special

You admire and hold this person in high esteem, giving her due recognition by enlarging her name. In your mind, she rises above others.

HIGH REGARD FOR THE OTHER PERSON

Dearest Adele,
I want you for my wife more than

You know he's there, but you'd like to cancel him out. You take any opportunity to run a line through him, either with a *t* crossing or with the stroke which ends his name.

SOMEONE YOU'D LIKE TO DESTROY

Hi Marty,
I was thrilled to hear from you

Normally clear-minded and unperturbed, as indicated by the rest of the script, you have doubts and confusion about the person to whom you are writing. When you approach the name your hand indicates the lack of assurance you feel.

CONFUSED FEELING ABOUT THE OTHER PERSON

Dear Barbara,
I'd like to welcome you to the family

The various attitudes and feelings described in the foregoing handwriting indices may be unconscious. When you examine your feelings further, you will find that there is no such thing in this reference as a slip of the pen.

You need only compare the size of the other person's name to how large you write your own name to learn how you size him up in relation to yourself. It will be apparent whom you admire more.

GREATER VALUE OF SELF THAN OTHER PERSON

Hello Jack,
your presentation was well done — — —
Robbie

YOU SEE YOURSELF AS AN INDIVIDUAL

When you were born you were given a name, which is referred to as your given name. It belongs to you only, independent of any family member both immediate or ancestral. It is your token of identity to others, and whether or not named after someone else, the name is now your property and distinguishes you as an individual.

A surname carries on a family line. You inherit it along with a background and tradition over which you have had no control, and this is what your surname represents to other people. When a woman marries, she is not only taking on someone else's name but also that of his ancestry. Your attitude of your own individualism is seen by where the focus of attention is stressed on the various parts of the whole name.

If you see yourself as an individual, the capital letter of the given name is written larger than the capital letter of the family name, attributing greater importance to the individual.

Louis Martin

You resent following in another's footsteps. Not only is the capital of the surname smaller than that of the given name, but the added ·burden of having to carry along a "Jr." is even less desirable, as indicated by its diminution.

Stanley William, Jr.

Here you attach greater importance to seeing yourself as part of a family than you do to being a separate individual. You are only important because you belong to them.

Marvin Morton, Esq.

A WOMAN'S FEELING OF IDENTITY

There are certain guidelines in analyzing the signatures of married, divorced, and separated women. Following these guidelines will give you evidence of a woman's attitude about the role she plays in society.

Consideration is given to the rules of how a woman is supposed to sign her name, depending upon her marital status. However, she frequently ignores these rules in preference to asserting her individuality.

Mrs. Richard Ainsley, Jr.

This widow not only holds onto her deceased husband's given name, but also to his family descendancy by maintaining the "Jr." in her own signature.

Mrs. Estelle Davenport

Using the proper signature form, this widow not only reduces the size of her given name but also has difficulty writing it, as though she would rather not.

Mrs. Alfred Tyler

The title of "Mrs." is significantly smaller and weaker than the husband's given and surname. He means everything to her and she's so grateful he married her.

Mrs. Anna Fairchild

The marital status is acknowledged, but without too much concern, as indicated by the casually written "Mrs." and husband's surname. The woman's given name stands out strong and clear, as marriage has not confused or distorted her self-image.

Stephanie E. Brockman

It is not unusual for men or women to drop titles when writing their signatures, but when a married woman not only drops the title of "Mrs.," but also reduces the size and space she gives to her husband's last name, you can be sure that's what she's doing in her marriage.

YOUR SELF-VALUE

The image you have of yourself has in good part been influenced by your belief of what others think of you and have thought of you in the past. It is a mature personality who can reconcile all the influencing factors and finally arrive at a comfortable and realistic acceptance of himself.

If you always wanted to live up to the expectations of others and never came close to it, you most likely value yourself with low esteem. If you failed to achieve the objectives you set for yourself and are unable to consider significant your small successes, this too would result in small self-value. Preconceived notions of inadequacy may have deterred you even from attempting to meet certain levels of performance, so that the poor self-image continues as this lack of self-confidence persists.

To understand your motivation today, you should go back and reflect on what motivated you as a child. You may have pursued a goal in order to get love and approval, without any appreciation for what you were pursuing. As an adult, you should reappraise the goals you seek, to be sure that you are not just pleasing a mother or father image, but because they now satisfy you personally. This will allow you a truer measure for self-worth.

This is a highly competitive society. You learn early in your life that most people judge you by comparing you to others. It is natural that you begin to judge yourself the same way, by comparative levels. First, your parents compare your behavior to your brothers, sisters, or neighbors. At school you are graded and evaluated on the basis of your classmates. At work you must do better and more than fellow employees in order to get ahead. In romance and marriage, competitive play continues in the game of wooing and keeping your fire brighter and hotter than others. In this environment it seems almost impossible for a personality to emerge free and self-realized. However, many well-adjusted people have learned to play the competitive game without letting it interfere with the value they have of themselves.

The letter *I* is a complete word, and though it is written frequently many people have difficulty expressing it in their handwriting. Direct and brief, it is the most highly personal one-letter word in the entire dictionary. From the way you write this one letter, whether as a word or part of a word, many of your feelings and attitudes about yourself can be determined. *I* refers to the self, the focusing point of your thought, so how you handle this ego letter-word will reveal your most personal feelings about yourself.

Satisfied with what you are, you state your *I* with simple direct assurance. You neither exaggerate nor reduce self-importance, and the letter *I* is consistent in style and size with the rest of the writing. Feeling secure, you have no need to convince others of your worth.

(a) *I find the work itself satisfying*

(b) *I invited the people I enjoy being with*

You are confused and have doubts about yourself. This causes you to be hesitant and constrained when attention is focused upon you, either by yourself or others. The first sample below shows the suppressing of yourself by narrowing the upper loop of the *I*, so no one can move in—not even you. The second sample reveals that you are not sure of yourself, because you hesitate and stop in the middle of writing the letter *I*.

(a) *I wish I could find an understanding*

(b) *I'm not sure I can handle the job.*

Your *I* is blown up and out of proportion with the rest of your writing. You spend a great deal more time and effort in trying to draw attention to your superficial self than to the value of what you do. An inflated ego is not one that is secure, for its hungry appetite can only be fed by constant attention from others.

I appreciate the compliment, but I know it's no more than five carats.

A feeling of being insignificant is often accompanied by an attempt to hide from others. You think little of your own importance; therefore, you write *I* small and obscure. To be sure that this is not just a subterfuge or pretended modesty see if the small *i* is also relatively smaller than the other letters.

a) SMALL SELF-IMAGE

I don't think I will be invited to the

b) PRETENDED MODESTY

I don't believe I'm qualified to do it justice.

An exaggerated self-importance differs from the inflated ego. You try to convince yourself and others by presenting your *I* in an exaggerated height. The doubt of confidence in your own importance may be that you are protesting too much.

I gave specific instructions that no

You have developed the belief that your worth can be measured only in relation to your importance in the society. You have no concept of a more personal self-value upon which you can judge yourself. The letter "I" conforms to the standard model, as you conform to the standard of the society.

I believe the committee requested that I

You repress your ego. There are things about your personal self that you will not look at, so you create a prison within which they are securely confined and out of public sight. These self-thought criminal characteristics have been shut in for so long that you may have forgotten all about them and are no longer aware that they even exist. However, your mechanism for guarding against their escape is almost automatic, for you keep them tied up so tightly that there is no way for them to become unbound. Unfortunately, innocent traits are also victimized because the ego is afraid of collusion and betrayal.

The *I* form is not only narrow in the upper loop, but the ending stroke ties up the letter in a knot. The writing slant is generally pulled backward in a posture of withdrawal.

I never in my life desired to do anything obscene, because I wasn't that kind of person.

Few people consciously try to damage themselves or destroy their ego. The accident-prone explain away their follies as carelessness or absentmindedness. The so-called born loser attributes his failures to bad luck, and many misfortunes are written off as the will of God. The question is how much of the ill fortune which may befall you is due to an inner self-destructive force? Here are some indications of that force in action.

Distorting the *I* changes its appearance so that it no longer resembles the original form. This is a form of self disfigurement. Further proof is evidenced when letters of the signature are also disfigured.

I simply don't know why I'm like this.
William Emory (William Emory)

You have written your name so many times in your life that spelling it correctly should be almost an involuntary action. When you misspell or misrepresent the important letters which identify your name, you are trying to destroy your image and are replacing it with something vague and undefinable—a self-disguise.

Mary Janes

Running a line through your *I* and signature is an act of self-obliteration or self-effacement—canceling out your existence. The inner urge to do this is equal to the strength of the line.

(Robert Henderson)

Your ego is free and unthreatened. You are open to yourself and others and enjoy the liberty of self-expression. You employ no guards to protect your ego, for you have no hang-ups about what you are and have no fear of reprisal from within and without.

Your *I* conforms to the true letter form in general movement and shape, but it swings freer and more openly. The upper loop is full and unsuppressed, and the entire letter character suggests a blithe spirit.

Self-Image Evaluation

If it were possible to make a generalized statement, which could apply to all individual personalities, about what is the most important step necessary to realize a happy life, this chapter would take priority. Your whole life is largely determined by what you think of yourself. Your whole life can be different by a reappraisal of yourself, without even making one physical change.

Approach this evaluation with an open, positive mind, for it is only valuable under this condition. It takes maturity and confidence to submit without fear and imaginary threats to a self-test of introspection. An aid to overcoming any anxiety is to separate yourself into two people. The one that answers the questions can be your less personal self, able to view both of you objectively. You can then reunite as one, with a much greater appreciation for the whole self.

WHAT YOU LIKE OTHERS TO THINK OF YOU

___ Outgoing and aggressive

___ Artistic

___ Modest

___ Important

___ More beneath the surface

___ Busy and active

___ Warm and compassionate

___ Cool and reserved

HOW YOU SEE YOURSELF

___ As an individual

___ Forced to follow another's footsteps

___ Living in shadow of family

___ If a woman, important only as a wife

THE STATE OF YOUR EGO

___ Secure

___ Insecure

___ Inflated

___ Small self-image

___ Exaggerated self-importance

___ Important only as member of society

___ Repressed ego

___ Self-disfigured

___ Self-disguised

___ Self-effaced

___ Free and uninhibited

It is suggested that you go back and compare your answers to the questionnaire on the first page of this chapter to check their consistency. If there are many differences, it is a sign that you are evaluating yourself with sincerity and expanding your scope for new attitudes.

11.

your total personality

Now that you have survived the rigors of exploring yourself in the most intimate corners of your personality, you can enjoy the reward of adding up these characteristics and be able to see the finished portrait. Don't be alarmed by a few misplaced brushstrokes, for you have been given sufficient testing to reflect your important features truthfully. With this valuable self-portrait at this present stage of your life, you have a more accurate mirror to look into now and in the future. Only you can judge the weaknesses, strengths, distortion, and beauty which look back at you, and only you have the special talent to develop this portrait further.

DISTINGUISHING THE SEXES

There is no sure way of determining from your handwriting whether you are male or female. The physical parts of your body do not reveal themselves, only the mind and emotions which make them function stand out naked. A man and a woman may play a different role in life, but when you reach the real human qualities of their being, you will find more similarities than differences. A man is truly a man when he can feel something of what a woman feels, for only then can he be a desirable lover and companion. Sensitivity and compassion are felt by a man for a woman because something in him identifies with her. This identification may be labeled a female characteristic, but it proves him more of a man in his relationship with a woman and with other men, who are truly men.

"Frailty, thy name is woman," was written demeaningly by Shakespeare. There is nothing weak or petulant about a real woman, once she rises above the role she believes she is supposed to play. Contrary to Shakespeare, it is having some of the endurance and strength generally attributed to a man which makes a woman a woman.

HOW TO EVALUATE YOUR TRAITS

Isolated characteristics are little more than meaningless, for they don't explain you or do you justice. However, they are highly valuable when related to one another, for then you can begin to understand why you think, feel, and act the way you do. For example, your emotional trait may be affectionate and sympathetic, your physical trait aggressive and forward-moving, your thinking perceptive and probing, but you register a small self-image. This gives you insight that your strong potential for successful performance is handicapped by an unwarranted low opinion of yourself. Probing even further may provide you with the reason, for if you have always been overshadowed by a member of your family, or family name and tradition, this could be the stumbling block you trip over.

Compare the traits carefully with each other, finding the reasons for your present attitudes and behavior. Consider the amount of energy you record in the physical and sexual traits and how you are presently using this energy. If your expression shows hostility and nervous anxiety, you know this energy is being diverted to less healthy channels. If you are imaginative with artistic potential, but are socially tied to convention, you will realize why your talent has not naturally progressed.

Be aware of yourself as both child and adult, and which one dominates the specific characteristics. You may be surprised to discover the number of traits which still cling to the child in you. This is your moment of revelation. Meet it head on with excitement and anticipation. Thus far you have kept an open mind. Don't stop now. This is the real beginning.

YOUR PERSONALITY PORTRAIT

The traits are listed as they appeared in the preceding chapters. Indicate below the graphological characteristics which you stated at the conclusion of each chapter. Your answers to the questionnaires at the beginning of each chapter were given only so that you could compare what you thought of yourself with what you discovered in your handwriting. Do go back to any chapter you wish in order to reclarify your findings. It's a lot to chew on.

1. Motivational Symbols

___ Love   ___ Security   ___ Sex   ___ Imagination

2. Emotional Traits

___ Affectionate and   ___ Cool and reserved
    sympathetic   ___ Alternately warm and cool
___ Warm and lovingly   ___ A loner
    responsive   ___ Withdrawn and unreachable
___ Leaning emotionally   ___ Emotionally confused
    on others

3. Physical Traits

ACTION SPEED: ___ Slow ___ Moderate ___ Fast ___ Racing

ACTION FORCE:
___ Dynamic ___ Strong ___ Moderate ___ Weak
___ Nonfunctioning

ACTION DIRECTION: ___ Forward ___ Neutral ___ Backward

4. Thinking Traits
   ___ Probing and penetrating   ___ Memory (good)
   ___ Concentrative ability   ___ Memory (poor)
   ___ Agility   ___ Anticipation (good)
   ___ Reasoning and logical   ___ Anticipation (poor)
   ___ Dependent (mature)   ___ Intuition
   ___ Dependent (immature)   ___ Organization (good)
   ___ Problem solving   ___ Organization (poor)

5. Social Traits
   ___ Extrovert   ___ Stubborn   ___ Ambitious
   ___ Introvert   ___ Yielding   ___ Lazy
   ___ Moral   ___ Resentful   ___ Proud
   ___ Amoral   ___ Compassionate   ___ Vain
   ___ Generous   ___ Inconsiderate   ___ Humble
   ___ Conservative   ___ Optimistic   ___ Self-Confident
   ___ Frugal   ___ Pessimistic   ___ Impatient
   ___ Humorous   ___ Shy   ___ Cautious
   ___ Witty   ___ Ostentatious   ___ Deceitful
   ___ Sarcastic   ___ Procrastinator   ___ Honest

6. Signs of Repression
   ___ Exaggerated imagination   ___ Suppression and canceling
   ___ Fantasizing   ___ Occasional reveries
   ___ Morbid fantasizing   ___ Conflict of past and future
   ___ Daydreaming   ___ Living in the past
   ___ Absentmindedness   (child ___ adult ___)
   ___ Canceling out   ___ Creative withdrawal
   ___ Suppression

7. Talent Potential
   ___ Art   ___ Science
   ___ Dance   ___ Architecture
   ___ Music   ___ Leadership / Organization
   ___ Creative writing   ___ Philosophy
   ___ Acting   ___ Spiritual leadership

8. Physical Problems

Body pain (Indicate area) _____

_____

Loss of or nonfunctioning part _____

Nervous disorder _____

Motor disturbance _____

Fatiguing illness _____

9. Sexual Traits
___ Hypersexual   ___ Romantic
___ Strong sexuality   ___ Conventional
___ Moderate sexuality   ___ Sensualist
___ Undersexed   ___ Sexually repressed
___ Total sexual   Withdrawal ___
      expression   Redirection ___
___ Incomplete sexual   Ambivalence ___
      expression

10. Self-Image
___ Secure   ___ Living in shadow of family
___ Insecure   ___ Forced to follow another's
___ Inflated ego   footsteps
___ Small self-image   ___ Repressed ego
___ Exaggerated self-   ___ Self-disfigured ego
      importance   ___ Self-disguised ego
___ Important only as a   ___ Self-effaced ego
      member of society   ___ Free and uninhibited
___ If a woman, important
      only as a wife

THE NEXT IMPORTANT STEP

Before rushing to the next chapter, list on the next page those characteristics you would like to change or develop further. Be sure you have spent enough time and soul-searching in the conclusions you have arrived at from this self-evaluation. You are diagnostician, adviser, and therapist, so treat your patient responsibly.

DESIRED PERSONALITY CHANGES—AND WHY

12.

how you can change

It has been said that the only thing that is really constant in life is change. Too many changes are brought about by circumstance and conditions over which we can contribute little and they are often not desired. Why then wait for something to happen, until your thinking becomes so sclerotic that it is inflexible to the idea of change?

The time is now and the concern is with one person—yourself, for nothing else will change around you unless you do. There are a few vital questions you must answer to your own satisfaction before approaching any metamorphosis.

1. What specifically do I want to change?
2. Will it make me happier in the long run?
3. Do I desire it enough to sacrifice something I have now and with which I feel secure?
4. Will I be able to face the effect a change in me will have upon others?

If you know exactly what you would like to change about yourself, and can answer "Yes" to the other questions, you have created the right atmosphere for realistic readjustment. If you are excited about the prospect, you are already beginning to feel the renewed energy which builds up within you when a new purpose comes into your life. Fatigue and vague illnesses will magically disappear, enthusiasm will replace the tension and pressure of getting through the day, and sleep will come only because the body needs it and not as a means of escape. When this happens, you'll know the change is right.

This chapter is so organized that you will have no trouble locating the characteristics you wish to change. It is suggested that you work with your personality portrait so that you will have an immediate picture of both conflicting and compatible traits. It is important that you read and understand the conditions necessary for change before you rush into the action, for they are an integral part of the change process, which will distinguish your move from just a sometime whim to a real and meaningful transition.

ESSENTIALS FOR CHANGE

People fail in their attempt to change because their desire is not followed by the practical process which allows change to happen. They may sincerely wish to be different, but they don't know where to begin. The characteristic you wish to alter must be clearly defined in your mind, as well as your reason for wanting to do so. This adds realism to the intention and removes feelings of desperation which produce an unfavorable climate.

Think about the years invested in the developing of your current personality traits. They also followed a pattern to make them what they are today, but you allowed them to happen because you were unprepared to prevent their taking hold upon you. You now have the opportunity to equip yourself with the tools of knowledge and emotional maturity to move toward change successfully. You are in control, and by understanding how you acquired your present traits, you will be able to make more gratifying replacements.

HABIT

A habit is an action pattern you acquire and continue to follow until it becomes almost involuntary. The longer the habit is in use, the more effort is required to change it. It may be a thought, a gesture, or a feeling which becomes attached and then part of the body system's functioning. No matter how undesirable this trait may be to its possessor, because it is so familiar it resists being ignored.

Habits are not changed overnight, but with the right approach the process can be sped up immeasurably, and you can be rewarded with beginning changes almost immediately. Circumstances sometimes create change in a person where there has been no plan to bring it about. I have seen a man change from arrogant to humble after surviving a critical illness, and this new attitude persisted in the years that followed. Shock, threat, illness, and drastic shifts in situation and environment often cause such changes, and they have proved worthwhile in the long run, but they are unpredictable and never without considerable sacrifice.

The best way to change a negative habit is to begin to replace it with something you feel is positive. This will buffer the loneliness caused by the disappearing old familiar trait and compensate with a new acquaintance who can really become a loyal friend. You may discover that you and the new trait are really not compatible, but at this point you can easily sever your relationship and search for a better companion. The progress you have made is in having begun to break away from the old, unwanted one.

The concept of compensation and replacement is used broadly in rehabilitative programs. The alcoholic is offered religion, the mentally and physically handicapped are given job retraining, the yogi suggests you replace the smoking habit with breathing in more air, replace excessive eating with drinking large quantities of body cleansing water, and throw out nervous excitement by replacing it with quiet meditation.

You do not need to comply literally with Socrates' "Law of Opposites," but only to consider that having lived so intimately with a trait for a long period of time, you might feel its loss strongly unless you have something else to fill up the gap. You needn't be the victim of compulsive behavior. Within the framework of your personality, you have the freedom to choose the habits to change and develop. Take advantage of that privilege; you have only everything to gain.

CREATING ATMOSPHERE FOR CHANGE

A new habit cannot begin to take place in the same atmosphere as the old one. That means that there is an attitude which surrounds a habit which keeps it safely fortified. A simple example is that of a round-shouldered person who has gotten that way by allowing his upper spine to curve forward. The idea affixed itself that this position was more comfortable, so he continued until slouching became a habit. In order for him to change to an erect posture, he must convert the old thought that slouching is comfortable to the idea that learning to stand straight will be more comfortable. A more dramatic example is the passive individual who wants to become aggressive. He has lived in an atmosphere of believing that he will fail at whatever he attempts. By replacing the atmosphere with thoughts of success, he is providing the conditions where action becomes less inhibited.

No one can be rehabilitated or redirected if he remains in the same neighborhood which caused the peculiarity to begin with. The juvenile courts are beset with the problem of returning minors to the homes where their problems originated. The old pressures and influences must be removd so that new habits have a chance to take root. One of the more common dilemmas is seen in the habit of argument. Two people are in constant battle with one another. Each has formed his own pattern of arguing and they stick to it until one relents from sheet exhaustion of spirit. Nothing is gained, no real satisfaction or victory won. How to change a habit of arguing? Easy, just investigate the true motives and place them in an atmosphere of reason.

What you are actually doing is moving your old habit to a new neighborhood where it no longer feels at home, and striking up an acquaintance with a new habit which can prove to become a loyal and lasting friend. Since you are looking forward to meeting and getting to know him better, invite him into your new surroundings.

REWARD

Regardless of your age or level of maturity, reward will nourish your incentive to change. There is no need to feel squeamish or insulted by the assertion that you, as well as all other people, expect a return for everything you do. It is as basic as the law of inertia, that for every action there is an equal reaction. Rewards are sometimes very subtle. A woman compliments her husband and feels a throb of elation when she sees his face light up. A father apologizes to his son and feels a greater love because he is able to do it. The son responds with warmth, delighted at the opportunity to forgive his father, and a closer bond is made between the two. A man contributes great sums of money anonymously. His return may be the satisfaction of helping worthy causes, a relieving of guilt, or just a tax write-off.

Everybody wants a reward, but everybody's idea of reward may differ. What is gratification for one, may be punishment for another, for people have had varying experiences where reward is concerned and have developed a concept of reward particular to themselves. Nevertheless, many individuals have reversed their likes and dislikes when conditions were conducive and the motivation strong. A man who has never wasted time in spectator sports becomes an avid enthusiast when his son makes college All-Star. A sun worshiper turns to loathing the sun after suffering a severe case of sun poisoning. Someone who has never appreciated music may get to love it after learning to play an instrument.

You can set your own reward for everything you do, as long as you see some value in your effort. It is naïve to believe that wealth, worldly success, and social position are not important rewards both to the inward and outward personality. However, they are transient, depending too greatly upon external conditions and other people. It is wiser and safer to set dependable rewards you know you can count on to see you through a purpose, and if desired, accessible to you throughout a lifetime.

Here are some rewards you might consider for your effort in changing a personality trait:

1. Adventure (excitement of a new image) .
2. Willpower (self-admiration) .
3. Projected successful results.
4. Greater recognition and approval (later, you won't need it) .
5. Sensation and pleasure (self-stimulation) .
6. Healthier body and mind (removing anxiety and body tension) .
7. Feeling free to be able to change.

You can find many personal compensations for yourself, but the greatest reward will come from actually enjoying the change.

State desired changes and the reasons for them.

CHANGING YOUR HANDWRITING

Mystery may be intriguing and romantic, but it is understanding and logic which give entrée to broader experience. There are no mysteries or gimmicks to changing your personality through handwriting. It is a sound and practical approach to positive self-programming. You keep feeding an idea into your conscious mind frequently and long enough for it to be transmitted into your unconscious level, for the cooperation of both are necessary before the idea can become affixed as a habit. The knowledge that a specific handwriting movement reflects the character habit you wish to develop is the key to making it happen. You change a particular characteristic of your handwriting, aware of its meaning and the reason for doing it. Every time you write this changed form, you are reminding yourself to think the new idea. Here you are reinforcing your thought with an action, the action of writing.

Every time you pick up a pencil or pen to write, you should alert yourself to the changes you wish to make. At first, it will seem difficult and unnatural. When you no longer have to think about writing these changes, but make them automatically, you'll know the actual personality characteristic change has taken place.

Use this book as your reference guide. You can find illustrations of traits you wish to avoid and also those you would like to develop. Here are a few to start you off:

Creating a Stronger Self-Image.   The following sample indicates a lack of self-worth. The *I* hides from the other less personal letters. The narrowness of the loop also restricts its freedom to express itself openly.

I can't ask for a raise. I don't even know if the boss likes my work.

Give your *I* the importance it deserves by making it larger and at least relatively equal to the other letters in the writing. Also, increase the space inside the loop so that you have more room to move within yourself.

I applied for the job. I think my qualifications...

More Resolute in Purpose.   Hesitation, being overly concerned with what people think, and impressionability deter you from your original purposes. Dashes are equivalent to spoken words which grope and hedge, like saying . . . well . . . uh . . . now. . . . Word-ending strokes show greater need to please others than to please yourself.

Well — if you really think I should - maybe

Now observe how just a few minor changes add firmness to the character of the writing, as it will to the character of your personality. The periods and *i* dots are strongly stated and terminal strokes end abruptly and adamantly.

I intend to do it no matter what anyone thinks!

Greater Objectivity.   If you are overly emotional, you respond more to feelings, leaving little room for reason. You give in to people easily, and are frequently taken advantage of because they recognize the vulnerability of your emotions. Your strong feelings interfere with qualified judgment and do not always work in your best interest. The slant in your writing is extremely forward, almost falling over itself in reaching out to others.

That's not much, only $5.00 a month for twenty years

Greater control and objectivity can be achieved by pulling back just a little. This will not disturb your naturally warm and responsive nature, but only afford you more emotional independence.

How much of that sum is actually interest?

Less Objectivity and More Natural Response. Just reverse the above process, allowing your slant to move a little more forward. As you extend your writing slant, so will you extend more of your personal self to others.

There is no danger in reserving the neutral slant when you wish to act with emotional detachment, such as taking notes, writing memos, reminders, and itemized lists. Here's an example:

1. Next week is the wedding
2. Buy a sheer black nightgown
5. Talk to Jay about honeymoon

But when you really want to feel close to someone, lean a little more toward him, like this:

I haven't a thing to wear for our honeymoon trip, sweetheart!

Greater Sexual Freedom. In comparing the handwriting of widows and widowers who have remarried, one of the most observable changes I have found is in their sexual expression. When the sexual activity was inactive or incomplete, the corresponding lower loops of the writing were also incomplete. If the length of the downward lower loop is long and strong, but does not return upward with similar intensity and completion, it is evidence that the sexual energy is being cut off. The force exists but is not being totally liberated.

Since my wife died, everything seems empty - - -

After remarriage, and a return to the more normal sexual state, these loops followed through to a happy, upward completion. The frequent reminder to satisfy your sexual needs more fully by completing these lower loops will remove some of your frustration, and also that of your mate.

Amazing, but marrying did has changed everything for me.

Setting Higher Goals.   Are you someone with talent and ability, who never seems to get anywhere in spite of it? You may attribute your state of mediocrity to "the breaks in life" or the burdening responsibilities which hold you back from realizing your true potential.

The naked truth is probably that you never stretched yourself high enough to reach the top of the mountain and sit there, but only viewed it from a lower level. The mountain is the *t* bar, and you stand just where you crossed it with your forward stroke.

If I put my mind to it, there isn't anything I couldn't do.

There is always an element of risk, but you have the tools for a higher climb and should strive higher upward. As long as the crossing stroke still touches the *t* bar, you are on sure footing. Even if you slip a little, it won't prove fatal, for you can easily regain your balance and footing with all the valuable equipment with you.

I'm not worried about the competition. Let them worry about me.

Removing the Fear of Beginnings. If you are afraid to begin something new, it will show by the undersized capital letters which begin a sentence, for it too is the beginning of a thought and action. Though you may move with greater ease and assurance as you become more familiar with what you are doing, you start out weak. The danger in being apprehensive about beginning something new is that it might deter you from doing it at all—and what a waste if timidity in starting off is your only handicap.

your approach him with the idea. whatever the outcome, I'll support you all the way.

Change to larger and more affirmative capitals, and this will remind you to approach your beginnings more aggressively and with greater confidence. You will begin to take advantage of opportunities that you shied away from before.

There's no risk until you fail. But there's also no success until you risk.

Unstifling Yourself. "Stone walls do not a prison make, . . . If I have freedom in my love, . . . And in my soul am free, ..." Richard Lovelace understood the deeper meaning of freedom. Most prisons are self-imposed, with the individual acting as a judge who sentences him to a life term. He then takes the role of guard, watching himself carefully so that he does not escape.

If you feel confined and inhibited, it is because you are not expanding the area in which you are now moving. This space may have been adequate when you were a smaller person, but the reason you need more room is because you are growing.

The sample below shows many chambers to the inner self, as revealed in the separating spaces between words, but the chambers are so small and narrow that it is difficult to breathe and move. Note how little space is used within the words themselves.

We visited all of Europe in two weeks, staying at the best American hotels and seeing all the most famous sights.

The writing may be large, but it is still stifled and crowded.

Our friends are the same people we knew 20 years ago.

Whether your writing is large or small is irrelevant. The change you must make is in taking longer steps from one letter to the next and making the letters more open. This is one of the most difficult traits to acquire, for it involves your whole pattern of moving in every phase of thought, emotion, and physical action. Many forgeries are detected because the forger has difficulty reproducing the same spatial relationships. Patience and perseverance will pay off, and when you actually begin to notice yourself swinging your arms more freely, taking bigger and easier steps, and saying things you never dared utter before, you will know you have emancipated yourself.

I'm interested in his ability, not his family background.

Loosening Conventional Ties.   Your desire to change this trait indicates that you are not tied to convention by choice, but by some compulsive need undoubtedly seeded in early youth. A tie to convention means being bound to it, rather than free submission. In following to a T every small rule of writing learned in early childhood, the implication is indisputable that you are shackled to early indoctrinated principles of right and wrong. You allow yourself no free interpretation, and, as the sample below indicates, your personal style is limited by the need to conform to the originally learned model.

Certainly I refused to have lunch with him. After all, I am a married woman.

You can begin to break off the ties by breaking off some of the strokes which connect one letter to another. You can also omit some of the beginning letter strokes, which wean you away from the absolute rule of thumb. These are small unconventionalities which in no way detract from you as a moral and responsible member of the community.

Well, perhaps one drink, but not here in public. How about your apartment?

Develop Greater Concentration and Memory.   Threading a needle does not require great mental acuity, but getting the thread through the eye of the needle does call for concentration. When looking at small print, you focus more attention on the reading material. It is technically more difficult to paint a small miniature than to work on a large canvas, just as a watch is more difficult to repair than a clock. Small movements require greater concentration than large ones, for they have to be more exact and better controlled.

When the overall writing pattern is large, the writer is throwing out his thought and action before he thinks them out carefully. He is anxious to express himself first, and maybe later work out the details. If he forgets to cross the *t*'s and dot the *i*'s, the chances are he won't remember to get to them at all. If the punctuation marks are placed haphazardly, he will forget just when he was supposed to do the things he planned.

We'll work out the details after the contracts are signed.

To develop better habits of concentration and memory, you will have to sacrifice just a little freedom, but it will result in more productive and enjoyable use of freedom later. Reduce only the size of the middle-zone letter forms, for this is the least subjective zone and will not disturb your own personal expression. Though reduced, they must still appear clear and definable, which will cause you to concentrate on your writing and remind you to concentrate on other things. Also alert yourself to go back and dot the *i*'s and cross the *t*'s, especially when they are at the beginning of long-drawn-out words.

All bids must meet the specifications.

Developing Stronger Willpower. Your willpower can be strong if you don't permit anything to shake or swerve it. A firm and direct punch is powerful, but if the arm is arched when it swings, a lot of the power will be lost. This happens when you cross the *t* with a shallow or umbrella-like curve. If the pressure is also light, it is a sure sign of weak willpower.

I might go to night school to get my deploma.

Practice controlling the *t* bar crossing so that it is straight and firm. Intensify the pressure, making the stroke darker and stronger, and you will be reinforcing your determination to build a stronger will.

Getting this degree means everything to me.

Removing Compulsive Frugality. The habit of being economy-minded to the degree that you measure the value of everything you get by how much it will cost you is always at the sacrifice of time, effort, and pleasure. When you compare these losses with what else you may feel you have gained, you must conclude that you have shortchanged yourself.

If you are compulsively thrifty, you use everything available rather than waste, making it last as long as possible. This corresponds to your use of space in writing. The writing may be large or small, depending upon other personality traits, but it will be squeezed and cramped with the attempt to get as much into the writing space as possible. The more the economy trait dominates, the less space will be left on the paper. Where one word ends, the next will begin, both margins will be narrow, and the writing will begin up near the top of the page and continue on close to the bottom. Frequently, both sides of the paper are used, economizing not only on paper, but possibly an extra stamp.

The dress is very beautiful, but I do have a nice one to wear to the party. I'm sure the store will refund my money. I've only worn it a few times.

Think recklessly and get generous with yourself. Begin with larger paper so there are wide margins. When you finish writing one line, force your pen to start the new line a little lower than usual, leaving more space between the two. After a while, concentrate on allowing more space between words and then between letters. You will never become extravagant nor a waster, so don't worry about going off the deep end.

The painting is by an unknown and not very valuable, but I certainly get a lot of pleasure from looking at it

Developing Positive Thinking. No matter how redundant, overpushed and overworked by any number of sales, success, and self-actualization courses, this is what it's all about. Present it to yourself any way you like, but get it going for you. To develop this habit, three major personal characteristics must be strengthened. They have been discussed previously, in separate chapters, but they are inextricably woven together when you take an action.

1. Strong self-image.
2. Will and determination.
3. Faith in humanity.

Number one is identifiable in the strength and assertiveness of the word *I* and the signing of your given name. The second will show in the firm and strong crossing of the *t* bar stroke. The longer the crossing, the greater the determination. The third and last is reflected by your degree of optimism. You cannot look forward to a future without faith in your fellowman, for you need him in order to realize yourself. Your line of writing climbs upward with enthusiasm and psychical energy. The *t* bar crossings follow this uphill movement. You look upward, think upward, and consequently move upward. You can't lose with this combination.

Here is an example of negative thinking. The writing line is pulled down by lack of enthusiasm, the *I* is insignificant and hiding (though a large *I* may be written to project a false image), the *t* crossing is strong but negatively downward, and the signature is an attempt to belie the true attitude, but betrays itself with a canceling line through it.

NEGATIVE THINKING

Please try to convince Steve not to go into business for himself. If I thought he could make a success of it I'd be all for it.

Estelle

POSITIVE THINKING

This is an opportunity we can't afford to miss. I know Steve will make a success of it!

Estelle

The contrast between the two is strong, yet only a few writing characteristics are different. These characteristics can change your life from a disillusioned, dull existence to an exciting anticipation of a life of pleasure and fulfillment.

Make a new friend of yourself.

13.

the backgrounds of graphology

In the days when the Romans were persecuting the followers of the new Christian religion, the Christian believers were forced to conceal their faith, for if they were discovered the penalty was imprisonment and possible death. When two Christians met, one would use his stick to draw this symbol in the earth (」). The other would then respond by placing his stick at an equal distance away from the angle of the form and draw this symbol (⌐). The two forms together made this sign (┼). They at once recognized and trusted each other, then quickly dusted off the evidence of their identity.

Though their purpose was to communicate their common belief, they were at the same time revealing much more about themselves by the way they made their mark in the ground. The fearless, determined Christian's mark would have appeared like this (」), possibly citing him as a leader. If the other Christian were afraid and insecure, his mark would have been made weak and wavering, like this (Γ) . An outsider could observe that the completed symbol was drawn by two different personalities, who could not help but reveal their separate emotions ($\perp$) .

The urgency to communicate ideas, thoughts, beliefs, and feelings is as old as man himself. There is much conjecture and theorizing about the paintings and drawings found etched on the cave walls of Altamira, in northern Spain, by the Reindeer men who lived more than 30,000 years ago. These remarkable pictures of deer, bison, mammoths, and other animals carved in rock were fortunately preserved by landslides covering the entrance to the cave. Perhaps our ancestor, the caveman, was unconcerned with preserving his history for future civilizations, but we do know that he found a way to express himself within the limitations of his environment. He experienced the same thrill of imprinting his mark on the cave wall as we do when signing our name to a creative piece of work.

From the Egyptian hieroglyphics (sacred writings) to the simplified cursive writing of today is the reflection of many cultures. Writing continued to develop in keeping with the need to maintain records of social and religious laws, trade transactions, political documents and proclamations, scientific discoveries, philosophies, and artistic expression. For many of these years, writing was the luxury of the privileged few, but in today's Western world, it is basic equipment for almost everyone.

Graphology started as a somewhat superstitious novelty. From the writings of an Italian physician, Camillo Baldo, who set up a system for judging a man by his handwriting, emerged an interested group of opportunists. Somewhere in the 1600s, traveling entertainers and magicians would amuse royalty and nobles by describing their personalities and making prognostications of their future from their handwriting. Perhaps they were intuitive or had some unconscious insight of graphic expression, but there was not enough serious research at that time for graphology to be considered more than entertainment. Unfortunately, there are still a few magicians and entertainers practicing such graphology today.

Many countries have since studied and developed sound principles and methods for evaluating personality characteristics. "Graphology" means the study of written forms, and two French abbés back in the 1800s who coined the word, Flandrin and Michon, were sincere in their efforts to connect the character of writing with the character of personality. After studying thousands of handwriting samples, they published their evaluations in *The Mysteries of Writing* and *The Practical Method of Graphology.*

Later pioneers rejected Michon's theories, which were largely based on a system of isolated signs and strokes. J. Crepieux-Jamin emphasized the concept of the Gestalt in the analysis of handwriting. Traits cannot be isolated, for all parts are important in their relationship to the whole. The contemporary, Werner Woolff, concentrated on general patterns of movement rather than individual marks. What was intrinsically weak about Michon's system of fixed signs was his attributing a particular trait to all people who made the same sign in their writing, without a combined evaluation of other salient expressions. This is like stating that all people who bite their fingernails are nervous. One may be nervous, another sensual, and still another may be without a nail clipper. But if they were all to bite their nails, grind their teeth, and also stutter, you could then assume them all to be nervous.

Alfred Binet, noted for research and development of intelligence testing, was stimulated into investigating the possibilities of determining various degrees of intelligence in handwriting. He publicly reported that both intelligence and honesty were reflected, and skeptics grew less skeptical with Binet's statement.

The German school was mostly scientific in approach and, undoubtedly, the greatest contributor to the field of graphology. A psychiatrist, Georg Meyer, conducted experiments with patients by having them write while in states of mania, elation, and depression. He asserted that you could not dependably examine a patient's mental condition without considering the character of the person. "Brain Writing" was the term which Wilhelm Preyer, a professor of physiology, used to describe the function of writing. He set out to prove that the brain did the actual designing, while the hand merely carried out the action. He demonstrated with a subject who had lost all his limbs by having the man write with his mouth. After a comfortable adjustment from hand to mouth writing was made, a comparison of the before and after writing revealed both patterns to be amazingly similar. When you think on this, it's really not a startling revelation, for everyone is aware that the brain is interpreter, teacher, and commander of the body. It did, however, urge others on to further research in the field.

Probably no one did so much to further and at the same time retard the development of graphology than the colorful young philosopher, Ludwig Klages. He combined his own laws and principles of graphology along with the works of other men, and his publications created abounding interest and enthusiasm in Germany. Though highly regarded, much of his work was infected with metaphysical theory of personality, which he stated in his writings in an unclear, confused stream of ideas. It was said of him that he regarded the mind as something which disturbs living. His philosophy was that feeling and soul were inborn, and the conscious mental function was imposed into life from the outside, and that the two were hostile to one another. Klages resisted clinical and experimental psychology as a part of graphological study and insisted that the use of psychometric devices, which measure pressure and writing speed, were not sufficiently valuable.

German neurologists, physiologists, psychiatrists, and psychologists continued to apply their specific skills to establish further a correlation between the mind and body and the writing phenomenon. Their contributions proved graphology a valuable diagnostic tool in fields of medicine, sociology, vocation, criminology, and industry. When Freud first pronounced that there was no such thing as "a slip of the pen," graphology surely had to be considered a branch of psychology.

Other significant advances led by Max Pulver were made in Switzerland. He was extremely engrossed in the study of the use of writing space and how it applied to the use of inner freedom and out-toward expression. The Institute for Applied Psychology in Zurich has trained many graphologists, thus having provided a qualified testing procedure which is more often used than the Rorschach. In Budapest, the Ministry of Education set up an institute of handwriting research, and much effort is directed in Hungary to the use of graphology in child behavior and development programs.

America finally came into the picture, picking up the thread of extensive network study and research pioneered across the ocean. The psychologists Gordon Allport, Philip E. Vernon, and June Downey were serious-minded, feet-on-the-ground experimenters. In 1933, Allport and Vernon reported on the studies they conducted at the Harvard Psychological Clinic. The ultimate conclusion they drew from their studies was that a person's gestures and his handwriting appeared to be expressed similarly in personal style, and that evidence indicates a relationship between outward expressive movement and the inner personality. The statements were guarded, but the implications that handwriting is consistent with the other expressions of an individual are strong.

Who can look at a Van Gogh painting without feeling the passion and inner turmoil of the artist? The imaginative daring of a Frank Lloyd Wright structure is undeniably characteristic of the man. The royal majesty of a Wagnerian opera shows the height of the composer's own self-esteem, and Chekov reflects humility and humanity in the compassionate writing and feeling for his characters.

Everything you do shows at least a part of you. Look at the handwriting and see it all.

appendix I

CASE HISTORIES IN THE FIELD OF EDUCATION

Ever since the launching of Sputnik in 1957, our nation's school systems have undergone a number of dramatic changes. One of these changes is the increased emphasis upon achievement, an attempt to have each child acquire a certain level of proficiency at completion of each school year. We believed that the only way to ascertain this information was through standardized testing to determine a child's exact level of achievement. As a result, educators and psychologists developed extensive batteries of tests designed to identify learning and emotional strengths and weaknesses of each child. The field of education is now inundated with tests.

Schools now engaged in testing programs have discovered large numbers of children (estimates are as high as 40 percent) whose actual achievement is far below what would be expected on the basis of their intellectual ability. There is a gross inconsistency between what these children can do and what they actually do in school. The children have been labeled learning disabled, dyslexic, perceptually impaired, or one of a host of other terms. Many of the widely used tests for identifying specific learning problems in children employ some sort of writing in this testing.

After reviewing the results of the extensive batteries of tests administered, we discovered this interesting phenomenon: children with reading

175

problems often do poorly in tests which require the use of writing. A large number of these children are diagnosed as having eye-hand coordination or visual-motor problems. This led us to the belief that by using only a few specialized tests rather than a large battery we could eliminate or significantly reduce some of the flaws in traditional testing programs.

The writers in the field of learning disabilities have pointed out that there is a distinct relationship between reading problems and a person's handwriting. As a result of our study of the work of MacDonald Critchley, renowned in the field of reading problems, we believed that the inability to write a legible word or sentence could be a form of learning disability. Critchley stated in his book *Developmental Dyslexia* that "less well known than the errors in reading are the disorders of writing . . . which are always considerable in cases of developmental dyslexia." Anna Gillingham, creator of the well-known Gillingham method, wrote that the largest group of disabled children are those whose difficulty in writing coexists with other problems. Dr. S. T. Orton in 1937 informed us that writing problems may not be accompanied by loss of other skills of the hand. Thus a person can have dexterity in manual skills but still show writing problems.

Based upon the extensive work in handwriting analysis completed in Europe during the past three hundred years and the work in progress here in the United States today, we were convinced that the analysis of handwriting could be a viable alternative in diagnosing children's learning and emotionally oriented school problems. As a result of the overwhelming evidence that our effort was justifiable, we engaged in a pilot project to discover whether examination of a child's handwriting could predict, with a high degree of accuracy, a learning disability and the nature of the disability. The children selected were diagnosed as having a learning disability. These students were asked to write two letters, over a period of two weeks, to a friend or family member and to sign his or her own signature to the letters. In general, these letters were friendly and informative without being very personal. They could not be judged by the teachers as having been written by children with learning and/or emotionally oriented problems.

The letters were then evaluated by Mrs. Solomon and the reports forwarded to the teacher. The teacher, on the basis of previous test results and her own knowledge and observation of the child, reacted to the graphological study of each child. The response was about 90 percent in agreement with Mrs. Solomon's evaluations and comments, and this was acknowledged to her with the mention of a few questionable areas. Mrs. Solomon sent a second report answering these points of question, which the teacher found to be clarifying and acceptable. She and Mrs. Solomon were almost in 100 percent agreement. Her reaction, as well as that of her aides, included such statements as:

1. "I'm totally sold; please evaluate my handwriting."
2. "Had I not read the reports with my own eyes, I never would have believed it!"
3. "Are you sure she has not spent many weeks working with these children, because I'd swear these reports could only have been written after extensive work with these children?"
4. "To think she has never seen the children, yet she knows them so well."
5. "I'm so excited with this new method of evaluating children because it tells us so much without having to expose children to all kinds of other testing."

I would like to outline briefly the reports on several of these studies. The children's names have been changed, but the cases are real.

Case 1: Sheila (age 7)

Graphological Report: Sheila is a fun-loving girl who generally speaks openly and frankly and is somewhat uninhibited. She is comfortable with numbers and is visual-minded with a good concept of form and shape. However, she has a constant need for reassurance which, coupled with what appears to be a hostile mother image, causes some intermittent tension and nervousness.

Teacher Comments: Sheila is indeed a "fun-loving" girl; however, the tension is present a good deal of the time, inhibiting this attitude, unless I continually tell her that the work she has completed is "good for her age." She is a very sensitive child and has many ambivalent feelings regarding both her mother and her sister, who is a year older than Sheila. I believe the hostility you noticed is directed more toward her sister than her mother. In fact, she recently told a student teacher that she did used to have a sister, but now she was dead. She speaks of her sister as being mean and unkind.

Mrs. Solomon's Answer: Hostility, in the mind of a child, is often unconsciously shifted from the parent on to a sibling. Frequently when a child is punished or not receiving the attention desired, the child will direct the antagonism toward another member, having been taught that you do not hate one's own parents. The desire to complete work that is "well done" may be indicative of insecurity at home. Her focus on numbers and quantities indicates that she has learned to be competitive, but needs to be accepted and loved when she fails.

Case 2: Bill (age 9)

Graphological Report: There is a problem of a disability in inter-preting (perception) the sounds he hears, or he suffers an actual hearing loss which should be evaluated by a qualified physician. He will forget things almost immediately after he has been told, or after he has said and done them. He lacks the ability to concentrate. The desire to express him-self to others and his poor auditory-motor coordination create a good deal of frustration and tension. He has a keen imagination and a strong urge to communicate pictorially, and should do well at art. Physically, he seems to be large, move awkwardly, and bump into things, for he has poor per-ceptual judgment in distance and depth.

Teacher Comments: There is apparently no hearing loss, but Bill definitely does have auditory learning problems. Extremely poor memory and inability to repeat things in order are just two ways this is shown. His emotions are often easily expressed, his excitement accompanied by his voice which gets louder and louder and his physical expressions are more pronounced. He is, however, generally a happy child and aware of his weak points. This awareness does cause a good deal of frustration.

Mrs. Solomon's Answer: I'm surprised that no mention was made of his artistic ability. It is quite apparent in the handwriting sample.

Case 3. Jean (age 10)

Graphological Report: This is a reliable and responsible child who will try her best to be cooperative. She is very aware of her environment and seeks social acceptance and approval. A healthy self-image exists. She is easy to relate to, will show her feelings outwardly, and generally has an uncomplicated personality. Jean has good visual learning ability, good eye-hand control, and is artistic in form, movement, and tempo. This reflects an inner emotional control. She is bothered by something con-cerning her feet or legs, and though she writes enthusiastically about horseback riding, she is very apprehensive. Her thinking is slow and im-mature. There is little determination or leadership quality, not even on a social level, and she will avoid anything competitive. Somewhat afraid of new challenges, she is at the same time sensitive and will tend not to show her rejection of strong physical activities. She has good manual ability and though artistic, she is not creative. Her natural, even, and consistent tempo of movement should apply well to music, dance (providing she is physically able because of feet problem) , and art. She should receive appreciation for progress made even at a slow rate.

Teacher Comments: Jean is indeed a friendly, cooperative girl. She is very easygoing and well liked by the other children. She is very competent in art activities and shows a good deal of patience in activities which involve fine motor skills. Jean is quite moody on some days and very happy on others, depending upon how her day has been success-wise. I agree that she does not show leadership skills with children of her own age group; however, this seems not to be so when she interacts with younger children. The report mentioned possible problems with feet. At the time the sample was written, Jean had blisters on her feet and was unable to keep her shoes on. I agree she may be afraid of new challenges in the area of physical education as well as in subject matter in schoolwork, and she makes no pretense at expressing her feelings about it. She is slow and immature in many areas, strongly rejecting new methods and materials, but after the initial reaction takes one step at a time and shows great patience learning a new task.

Mrs. Solomon's Answer: The teacher's remarks are so consistent with the graphological report that there is little need for further comment.

The above outlines of three cases are representations of the power of the science of graphology. My intention has been to provide you with a sense of the relevance of handwriting analysis from the perspective of an educator and how it can provide an insight into a variety of problems. In this book, Mrs. Solomon has brought to you years of training, experience, and insight with the hope that you will come to understand yourself a little better. Hopefully, you will come to appreciate, as I have, the contributions and knowledge which Mrs. Solomon has synthesized in this salient book.

Robert S. Sloat, Ph.D.
Associate Professor of Education,
Florida Atlantic University

appendix II

CASE HISTORIES IN THE FIELD OF
JUVENILE DELINQUENCY

As a juvenile court judge, I am constantly seeking better ways of evaluating the backgrounds and character traits of those who appear before me. For this reason I have utilized social investigations, psychological evaluations, school reports, and community agency information.

When Shirl Solomon first discussed with me the possibilities of handwriting analysis in evaluating juvenile personality, I was intrigued. Surely, I thought, if perceptive, it could be of immense help as an objective and expeditious evaluation, not only for myself, but also for counselors and probation officers who worked directly with these young people.

On an experimental basis, I sent Mrs. Solomon a number of handwriting specimens of juveniles. In every case nothing was sent but the writing samples themselves, although occasionally some subjective information was revealed by the writer in his communication. When Mrs. Solomon submitted her analyses, they were checked against available psychological and social evaluations. It soon became obvious that handwriting analysis was an effective tool of evaluation, and in many cases even superior to other evaluative methods, because it can be more objective. Mrs. Solomon knew nothing about the subject except age, sex, and whatever information was included in the specimen. With parents and school authorities there is always the possibility of bias, and even the psychologist often bases his evaluation on his subjective observation of the subject's actions and statements. Since the physical presence of the person analyzed through handwriting is removed, it is much more difficult to distort his personality than by an interview with a counselor or psychologist.

One of the major problems faced by the juvenile court is in the decision to return a young person from a correctional detention to the environment of his home. In the case of a fifteen-year-old girl who repeatedly ran away from home, spending a few nights with a young boy, and considered beyond parental control, I sent for graphological study a sample of the mother's handwriting. The concluding remarks were as follows:

> The traits are so contrasting between mother and daughter that neither is able to identify with the other. The mother, though capable of understanding, does not have the patience nor the desire to sacrifice as much time of herself as a girl like W—— requires. She resents the constant impositions and setbacks to her own movements and will eventually grow to hate the girl if it continues. It is particularly onerous to her, as she admires all the qualities she possesses and is appalled by the lack of them in her daughter.

Comparing the analyses of both the child and the mother offered an added insight to the home situation and the influence of the mother's attitudes upon the behavior of her daughter. The girl ultimately ran away with her boyfriend.

One child who was before me for incorrigibility and sexual promiscuity recently became active in a church that catered to young people and which was unusually expressive and emotionally charged. Her handwriting revealed the following:

> She moves and leans inward and in the opposite direction of the society. Extremely emotional, her concern is only with self. She is not particularly suppressed or inhibited about her private doings, but with the outside world she is afraid and restrained. She fears the future, hides from it, and prefers the past rather than face what's ahead.

This same girl was described in her social case study as a "great prevaricator . . . one never knows when she is telling the truth or when she is lying. The thing that is so striking about this is J—— lies about insignificant things. She is overly dramatic and tends to overdramatize everything."

Her handwriting offers this additional insight into her proclivity to manipulate and fabricate:

> Though she thinks little of others, she thinks less of herself . . . all beginnings are difficult, so she reduces them in importance, avoiding them because she doesn't feel capable of doing anything significant . . . she is aware of obligation and responsibility, but is antisocial and will not respond to social demands, and will indulge in self-pity and remorse for her plight.

The question is whether she is lying as a result of typically simple manipulative tendencies, or is it the result of a considerable unwillingness on her part to accept reality (or truth-telling) , as revealed by her handwriting? The psychological evaluation is consistent with the handwriting analysis which reads, "Her performance or manipulation was only slightly higher than her verbal facility. . . . Qualitative analysis of her responses showed impulsivity, aggression and several dependency needs may color her thinking and behavior."

An interesting case is one of a seventeen-year-old girl charged with possession of alcohol, drug use, and immoral behavior. She was considered to be beyond parental control and dangerous to her own welfare, for she attempted to commit suicide by taking an overdose of nonprescriptive x-tension tablets. Here are some of the graphological comments based on the study of her handwriting:

> A—— is extremely sensual, harboring all kinds of physically sensating desires which she believes are unclean. She engages in excesses of thoughts and/or acts that give physical satisfaction, and reveals signs of wanting to become pregnant and carry a child . . . She believes her physical desires are base and dirty and, therefore, she is. Her intellect will not allow her to consciously accept this, so she sublimates by trying to induce loftier thinking. Aiding her to this aim is the use of drugs. She feels empty and alone. The desire to become pregnant is interwoven with wanting to fill up the gap, to become the child again and to have an object of love. She is involved with the concept of "love" and, wanting desperately to feel it, searches for an understanding. The resources she has for identifying with it are unreal and desperate.

Despite a long history of scholarly interest and acceptance of the basic premise of graphology, it has not yet been given its full due as an analytical technique useful to courts and agencies. My limited experience causes me to temper my enthusiasm and to reserve any judgment of its ultimate merit, but I am convinced that further scientific experimentation would establish graphological analysis as a valuable tool for courts and agencies.

Lewis Kapner
Judge of the Juvenile Court,
West Palm Beach, Florida

for further reading

Allport, G. W., and Vernon, P. E. *Studies in Expressive Movements*. New York: Hafner Publishing Co., 1967.

Freud, Sigmund. *The Psychopathology of Everyday Life*. New York: Macmillan, 1914.

———, and Breuer, J. *Studies on Hysteria*. New York: Avon, 1966.

Gesell, Arnold. *Infant Development*. New York: Harper & Bros., 1952.

Gregory, R. L. *Eye and Brain: The Psychology of Seeing*. New York: McGraw-Hill, 1966.

Harrower, Molly. *Appraising Personality*. New York: Franklin Watts, 1964.

Jersild, Arthur. *Child Psychology*. Englewood Cliffs, N.J.: Prentice-Hall, 1960.

Kohler, Wolfgang. *Gestalt Psychology*. New York: New American Library, 1947.

Krafft-Ebing, Richard von. *Psychopathia Sexualis*. Translated from 12th German edition. New York: Stein & Day, 1965.

Laing, R. D. *The Divided Self*. Chicago: Quadrangle, 1960.

Lucas, De Witt B. *Handwriting and Character*. Philadelphia: David McKay, 1923.

McMurry, Robert N. *Handling Personality Adjustment in Industry.* New York: Harper's, 1944.

Montagu, Ashley. *Man: His First Million Years.* Cleveland: World Publishing Company, a Signet Science Library Book, 1962.

Ogg, Oscar. *The 26 Letters.* 2nd. ed. New York: Crowell, 1961.

Pulver, Max. *Max Pulver's Symbolism in Handwriting.* Condensed and translated by Felix Klein.

Roman, Klara G. *Handwriting: A Key to Personality.* New York: Farrar Straus, a Noonday Press book, 1962.

Sonnemann, Ulrich. *Handwriting Analysis.* New York: Grune & Stratton, 1950.

Woolff, Werner. *Diagrams of the Unconscious.* New York: Grune & Stratton, 1948.

index of handwriting samples